How To Analyze People: The Ultima

Psychology Guide : Think Like A Psychologist

Influence Anyone, Learn How to Read People

Instantly, And Understand Dark Psychology

Introduction

This is your ultimate guide for understanding human psychology, behaviour, body language, theories, dark psychology, influencing people and personality types. What is the first thing that comes to mind when I say "psychology"? Your probably think of a shrink or a patient at a psychiatrist's office getting therapy. Perhaps you imagine a person's brain and the many intricacies, labyrinths, layers, consciousness and even sub-consciousness.

In short psychology can be defined as the scientific study of the human mind and how it functions in context. The mind is not tangible like our brains however, it can be thought to be of a more abstract and metaphysical theme that exists conceptually. The mind is governed and regulated via hormones which turn into thoughts. Our ability to think and reflect is what separates us from animals in the wild! Animals survive based on instinct alone and have a certain degree of collective efforts, but pale in comparison to a human's ability to reason, collectively work together, and pass on knowledge from generation to generations.

The mind is fertile ground that is continuously influenced by social surroundings, and this means from the day of your birth you are influenced by your context. What does this mean? From family, friends, school, religion, media, societal norms, cultural themes, and even peer pressure! Humans are impressionable beings meaning for the most part your upbringing taught you how to think and not even question it. People in authoritative positions most likely delegated your thought process and controlled, and even restricted information that you should be exposed too.

Think about it people in positions of authority or authoritative figures determine what is "right" versus what is "wrong" in the society we live in, and these people are usually the ones who hold the power and delegate from the top down. How do we determine if one strays off from the right path? – Laws, policies, and other international regulations are all social constructs designed by people in power to keep them in power. Laws are put in place to control the masses (99%) of the population and protect the 1%.

This is how its always been even since ancient times. There were always hierarchies, government bodies and social prestige all guised under the pretext of politics. Religion was another way people from ancient times controlled the masses, and due to lack of education for the average person back then people had almost no choice but to listen and follow orders or risk being exiled and outcasted.

The purpose of this book is to make you question prevailing ideologies, thinking and social norms. And to teach you how to analyze people, understand psychology deeper, grasp body language and personality types. At the end of this book I want you to be a critical thinker and as the great philosopher *Socrates* once said to his students *"question everything"*.

There are various nuances to human psychology, but over the centuries psychologists, philosophers and other great minds alike have broke down the fundamentals of human psychology. Humans beings operate under power, status, purpose and belonging (social solidarity). The break down is quite simplistic, however, if you look at historical events, famous figures, and other societal norms you can see these elements at play.

Power

Throughout history we can see the bloodlust power struggle from many conquers, tyrants, and bureaucrats. From the Mongolian emperor *Genghis Khan* who conquered modern day Russia, China, Korea, Persia, parts of India, and some of eastern Europe which drastically reshaped the world's geography, culture and history which still echoes today.

Alexander The Great was another mighty conqueror who invaded the Persian empires, India and Egypt. Till this day Alexander is considered one of the greatest and fearless military commanders who walked the face of the planet and is world renowned.

Lastly, I'd like to mention the *British Empire which was* the most successful military camping and conquest to date. British influence and customs primarily through the "English" language has been adopted worldwide from North America, Europe, Africa, India, Middle East, Mexico, etc. The British Empire was one of the biggest if not the largest empire that has ever existed and till this day still influences the many countries it conquered. The British Empire used the most strategic warfare tactics to essentially conquer the world. There was a saying that "the *sun never sets on the British Empire*" because of the sheer span of this kingdom which stretched from Africa, Asia, India, and even the middle east.

Now what do all these empires and leaders have in common? The answer is simple we can see a yearning hunger for power which caused many wars, exploitation of natural resources and humans, and countless innocent lives lost in the name of "power". This is a fundamental cornerstone of the human psyche and history tells the story well as we can see by observing past accounts. -The appetite for conquest, submission and ultimately power is clearly seen.

Status

Have you ever stopped to consider why people choose a particular brand over another? Or Perhaps why people drive certain luxury cars over others? The answer is status. Cars serve as a symbol of status to onlookers and being affiliated to a certain brand name product whether that be Polo, Nike, Reebok, Prada, Chanel, Armani, Gucci, or Louis Vuitton sends out a message to your peers.

The desire to acquire a higher social status appears to be a built in drive humans have had even since ancient times. Through clothing, cars or even the type of house we own all stem from the theme of status. In modern day society people want to be associated with the "middle-class status" because it has become the more socially acceptable norm and its neither looked down upon like those living in poverty or envied like those who are considered elite or wealthy.

This ongoing theme to prove-self worth and vanity goes even further than in person interactions but can even be seen on social media. Whether its Facebook, Instagram or Snapchat we can this see especially with the *millennial's* generation as they tend to be more tech-savvy but nonetheless the drive to flaunt status can be observed. Whether its a post of a picture taken with a famous celebrity, physique vanity, new car or perhaps the party scene. We can observe the desire to promote one's status from all angles originating from our built in drives as human beings.

Purpose

Purpose or reason of existence is a deep subject matter that almost every human contemplates at one point in their life. Having a purpose fills in the void of meaninglessness and enables humans to live a life filled with abundance, adventure and fond memories. Life is a gift and its up to us as human beings to embellish meaning and figure out our unique purpose here on this earth by discovering who we are and what value we have to offer and bring into this world.

A theme that has been debated for centuries by many great philosophers, poets, psychologist and great minds alike. A poet by the name of "*Catalyst*" also known as "*Poet-Memories*" once said "Having no purpose can be likened to a flower with no fragrance, and thus its up to every person to find their own unique scent by searching for it. "He goes on to say in his text;

Excerpt:

"I cannot walk this earth like a flower with no fragrance,
  No sweet aroma, no purposeful existence.
  So, I go on this expedition like a vagabond
  In pursuit of this elusive and soothing fragrance….."

-   **Catalyst**

Discovering our reason of existence is the height of human enlightenment and the epitome of becoming self-aware. Human beings thrive on having purpose which without would make life quite boring. Essentially figuring out your *why* is what keeps people going, but "purpose" differs from person to person and it can range from having a significant other, taking care of the kids, friends, family, financial feats, personal goals and even more altruistic reasons. Some "purposes" are more self-centered while others are more complex and altruistic, but nonetheless humans seem to thrive when they discover their unique and true meaning to life.

Belonging (social solidarity)

Having a belonging also known as social solidarity is similar to purpose but on a more collective scale. *John Donne* once said, "*No man is an island*", and in this simple yet concise piece of text a profound truth arises. The fact is humans are social creatures and thrive on social interactions, and we cannot dispute the fact that humans are dependent on each other for our very existence. The very act of "procreation" one of the greatest gifts of life fundamentally requires two beings to create a new life form.

History shows the power of unity and humans' capacity to work collectively together as a unit for the greater good of society. People want to belong and find unity, fellowship and ultimately a safe haven for oneself. This ties into status and even power because these attributes sort of overlap when you really think about it. Sometimes people may acquire power or status because they want to belong! -By holding power and status you tend to attract others and thus you establish an affinity to your peers and ultimately create a belonging.

Individualistic Societies (Capitalism)

Here in North America we take up central individualistic philosophies that govern the societies we live in. Emphasis is put on you as an individual and how you can be a contributor of society. Capitalism in essence is based on individualistic themes and ideologies which has created the economic environment we see today. There are pros and cons to capitalism just like any prevailing ideology, but clearly the pros appear to outweigh the cons for it to have existed this long and be promoted institutionally.

Capitalisms breeds innovation, incentive and a competitive edge that communist based societies don't have. Basically, establishing a free market where everyone has access to take advantage of and get ahead in life, although it must be noted not everyone is necessarily given an equal chance to climb the ladder as socio-economic status, generational wealth, and individual skill set all play factors in the success of a person. However, this model does reward those who are able to successfully take advantage of the free market and gives little room for government intervention and regulation.

Collective Societies (Communism)

Collective societies on the other hand such as Cuba, China, and North Korea have their own set of rules, philosophies and regulations when it comes to national sovereignty. These societies are heavily regulated and don't have a free market access like the western part of the world. Government rule plays a huge part into the day to day lives of people and their collective efforts for the greater good of society.

With communism the government distributes rations to its members accordingly, however this greatly limits the scope of entrepreneurship, progress, free market access and incentivized growth. With so much absolute control and *iron fist* ruling this makes economic growth difficult and has a trickle down effect to society's members which can greatly impact the lives of millions negatively. By disallowing incentives or rewarding entrepreneurship (found in capitalism) this can be quite detrimental to a nation's progress in the modern world. Corporations who find no benefit from capitalistic rooted policies to do business in a state or nation will simply look elsewhere leaving thousands of people unemployed which would greatly affect any economy adversely.

Chapter 1: Body Language Fundamentals

It is known fact that 80-90% of our communication doesn't necessarily come from what we say, but our body language and the context its in is what determines the message. Tone, cadence and how we deliver the content of our message to the recipient also plays a role in this as well. For instance, in one of my earlier books on facial profiling I used the famous painting of "*Mona Lisa*" as an example and pointed out that from her broad smile you cannot definitively determine if she is happy or not. Without observing the context of the situation and studying it thoroughly you can't tell if it's a bitter smile, showcasing shrewdness, reflecting cynicism, peculiarness, genuine joy and the interpretations of this historical painting can go on and on.

Hence, the importance of understanding body language and the context of the situation at hand to grasp a more comprehensive conclusion. Through comprehending body language cues, we can better understand the motives people try to either intentionally mask or explicitly convey.

Evolutionary Psychology

There is a region of our brain considered to be the more "reptilian", part of this region is known as the brain stem, which is responsible for making instant judgements of the people around us based on particular sets of behavioral traits. Our thought process goes something like this "should we approach this person will he or she be beneficial to us or shall we refrain from interacting because they are harmful to our well being?"

There are 4 fundamental categories that our brain compartmentalizes interpretation of both body language and the content of the message. These four categories are 1. Friend, 2. Enemy, 3. Potential sexual partner, and 4. Indifference. You can call these 4 categories built in drives within our brains that we have been utilizing for our survival for over centuries.

I'll elaborate on how exactly these 4 drives work in a practical setting. You're at a party and you somehow strike up conversation with another individual it could either be male or female this is arbitrary. Now these drives operate on a sub-conscious level, thus you may not be self-aware that you are executing these internal drives and functions. So, as the conversation is being kindled automatically your thinking is this person a friend based on posture; is this person using open, warm and welcoming body language, tone, cadence and of course is the core content of his or her message something that resonates with you. What your brain starts to do sub-consciously is it starts cherry picking reasons, past records and other accessible information and starts to reinforce favorable reasons why this individual you are conversing with should continue to be categorized as a "friend", contingent on if the body language and context of the entire message is received favorably.

Vice-versa on the other side of the spectrum is the person you have now engaged in conversation an enemy? Has this individual displayed repulsive body language, perhaps bad odour, rude tone, degrading terminology and an abhorrent message. The 3rd category as potential sexual partner can be triggered by our built in drives as well and this can be because the person your engaging exhibits appealing physical attributes, masculine or feminine characteristics, good hygiene, wealth, resources, social capital and perhaps a good sense of style.

Lastly, our 4th internal drive that can be activated sub-consciously is "indifference". Imagine being in conversation with someone whom you for some reason decided is not your cup of tea, and thus you filter them out by ignoring their advances. Generally speaking the vast majority of people from a psychological stand point are operating on the built in drive of indifference, simply because there are 7 billion people on planet earth, thus in order to capture your attention there needs to be some sort of appeal or reason for interest.

What Is Non-Verbal Communication? (Body Language)

So, what exactly is non-verbal communication? Its anything that encapsulates or conveys a message but not in words, however it manifests in our body language, tone of voice and contextual situation. Everyone utilizes non-verbal communication daily whether you are cognizant of this or not. Something as simple as your sense of style or the way you dress is a form of non-verbal communication. By dressing a certain way, you are conveying to your peers perhaps cultural affinity, social status, wealth and even power.

An interesting study revealed a political debate going on between two elected candidates, and viewers who listened by radio suggested candidate (A) won, yet viewers who watched by television stated candidate (B) was victorious. As you can see there is a bit of conflictual data here, but why is this happening? The simple answer in short is non-verbal communication or body language is what gave viewers who watched on T.V a different interpretation than those who listened in on radio!

Although, candidate (A)'s arguments were consistent, valid and transparent this individuals body language showcased something else. Candidate (A) revealed low self-esteem and the lack thereof confidence through poor posture and weak delivery of the message, while candidate (B) through body language conveyed alpha male status, dominance and a clearly conveyed message. As you can see the importance of body language must not be underestimate because on a sub-conscious level, we are interpreting everything that goes on in its context, so if you showcase weak body language your message may not be as impactful as someone who delivers with powerful non-verbal communication cues.

The interesting thing about reading or analyzing body language as a human being is that we all do it on a sub-conscious level. We all participate in analyzing our peers from the way they look, dress, demeanour, what they drive, their accent, etc. This all occurs rapidly and is second nature to us because that is the way humans have evolved socially over the centuries. Thus, the art of analyzing body language is not foreign at all, but something humans have always been doing on a sub-conscious level since ancient times.

Its quite amazing how much body language plays an integral role to our interpretation of certain events and the fact that body language really makes up most of our communication today. See below things that can simply be observed by analyzing body language:

Things Observed Through Body Language:

-Danger

-Emotions

-Desires

-Insecurities

-Manners

- Skill

- Personality

Danger – Have you ever gone to an ATM perhaps at odd hours maybe at night or even during the day. Chances are if you've ever withdrew a large amount of cash subconsciously your mind is telling you that there could be potential risks associated with you carrying such a big amount of cash on you. So, naturally you probably turn over your shoulder and look side to side, and even utilize security mirrors to check if there are any threats present that may put you in danger.

Emotions – Someone recently got married and is 2 months pregnant you can probably imagine the joy this woman would be expressing, high pitched voice, cheerful tone, excitement in conversation, welcoming body language and of course the universal trademark to happiness; the smile.

Desires – Body language for desire can come any many forms depending on the situation you may find yourself in. Imagine you're on the beach and you see an extremely attractive male or female (depending on what your sexual orientation is) the first natural inclination for most people would be a "double take", and than a long glance. Depending on your comfort level and confidence you may even approach that attractive mate and decide to talk to him/her. This type of desire is more of one seeking companionship and a potential sexual partner.

In another situation a fancy sports car drives by you, perhaps a blue colored *Huracán Lamborghini.* Your first reaction would be similar to the previous scenario, double take followed by a long glance. But obviously in this case your desires are different as the motive for a sports car is different than a sexual prospect. Your desire for a sports car ties into wanting to have a symbol of high status and garner respect from others.

As you can see desire can manifest in different shapes and forms, but the context of the situation will reveal the type of desire a person has.

Insecurities - The truth is everyone has insecurities, and nobody is immune to this. Regardless of how confident, how good looking, how much money, and the amount of social capital one has there will always be a certain degree of insecurity. The difference is that one's insecurity will vary from person to person, and people posses them for different reasons.

For instance, a teenage girl who is plagued with chronic acne constantly looks at the mirror to check up on her blemishes and covers it up with makeup. This behavior indicates the young teenager is insecure about how she looks, thus she must cover up her perceived imperfections because by the standards of society she must have flawless skin. Guys are not immune to this and are equally susceptible, and this could be acne too, body image, height, etc.

The feeling of inadequacy is natural human tendency because its in our nature to compare ourselves to others, and media magnifies this effect one-hundred fold. By promoting hyper sexualized figures who are not remotely realistic to what an ideal male or female body image should look like.

Manners – Manners differ from culture to culture depending on what side of the globe you find yourself at. But for this example, let's look at some body language here in North America. Imagine your in conversation with someone and although your captivated and giving your undivided attention to this person your engaged with, he does not feel the same way, thus he pulls out his phone while your talking and starts texting his other friends. Obviously, this is clearly a display of rude body language signified by indifference, not interested and probably means "can you stop talking to me" too. I'm sure we've all experienced this rude behavior at some point in our life in the 21st century now that everyone has a smart phone!

While on this subject of phones I wanted to add another interesting behavior that uses looking at your phone screen or using it as a pretext to mask "awkwardness". This is actually quite an interesting phenomenon that occurs socially, and I am more than certain you've seen this before. Perhaps you're at a party, bar, club or even outside in the public waiting for a bus. People seem to instantly draw out their phones as if they have something urgent to attend too. Although I'm sure some people actually have important things to do, but the majority of people who do this tend to exhibit this "look at phone screen" behavior when they feel awkward.

From a psychological perspective this usually happens when there's no emotional connection to the people around you, and thus you become indifferent towards them and instead of looking at the floor or wall awkwardly your go to strategy is to pull out your phone that way you can save face and look "cool" while doing it.

Skill- Skills is an easy body language to pick up on. If you watched televised sports whether that be hockey, soccer, basketball, golf or even foot ball you've most likely witnessed body language from athletes that reveal their competence or skill level. Have you ever seen the basketball player Lebron James walking down the court with squared shoulders, head held high, and glaring eyes? Compare him to the average basketball player in the NBA and you'll see a huge difference in demeanor and how they carry themselves out.

Lebron James is clearly one of the all time greats, and his body language reveals his confidence in his particular skill set and athleticism. The same goes for any other sport too. Even in a no-contact sports like golf, Tiger Woods expresses the exact same behaviour which reveals dominance, confidence and alpha male status.

Personality – Body language can reveal your personality too! You see body language is just a manifestation or expression of how you truly feel deep down inside. Imagine your in a subway you see an individual with his hands in his pocket, deep in thought, squinted eyes and closed off shoulders. You know right off the bat this is not someone you want to approach and you know this within in seconds because of the body language being displayed. On the other hand, if you saw someone with a pleasant smile and open stance your most likely going to approach this person for directions versus the other one.

Even the subtlest things can reveal your personality type, for example have you ever seen people on the streets literally "bull-doze" you down to the side without a second thought? They give you no eye contact whatsoever but look afar and walk right through you as if you're not present. This type of body language reveals passive aggressive behavior and chances are the person who does this has some aggressive tendencies and is someone you want to avoid.

Importance of Recognizing Body Language

By now you probably know that body language says a lot about an individual. There's a saying *"A picture is worth a thousand words" coined by Fred R. Barnard*, and this is a truth that is indisputable because people are more inclined to judge you based on your body language before they take your words at face value. For instance, you get into a heated debate with a friend on a controversial topic, and you tell your friend to calm down, but your friend states "I am clam!" yet displays body language including tone that says otherwise. Here is a classical example of someone saying something but their body language tells a completely different story.

Below are hallmark signs of pacifying behaviors revealed through body language:

Biting Lip – This action is actually an evolution of past behavior of what we use to do as babies. When we were infants, we "sucked our thumbs" and we did this as it was comforting to us. However, since its not socially acceptable for any sane adult to suck their thumb we instead bite our lips. This is our way of reliving stress the same way babies do, but without the thumb sucking.

Grasping face with two hands – Have you ever received bad news or perhaps you've made a serious mistake at work? Your first reaction was most likely to grasp your face, and this type of body language reflects both regret and distress, thus by quickly grasping your face it is your body's way of sub-consciously easing your stress.

Pull fingers or cracking knuckles – Are you or do you know anybody who has the bad habit of cracking their knuckles and pulling their fingers? Cracking knuckles is more common than pulling fingers, but the message behind both these actions are the same. This habit is also formed to pacify your stress and is a way you find comfort. Sometimes cracking knuckles can signify the start of a new arduous tasks or even the completion of a certain tasks.

Restless legs (shaking leg) – I'm sure you've experienced this at some point in your life or you've seen someone exhibiting the "restless leg syndrome". This usually indicates anxiety and by bouncing your leg up and down this is your body's way of calming you down and relieving your stress sub-consciously.

Pulling Hair – Now this is considered a more extreme form of pacification but is nonetheless body language for "I am stressed", and in this case your hair serves as a "punching bag" or stress ball that receives the full blunt of your attack. Simply put people who pull their hair are looking for ways to relieve their stress fast in that moment and thus use the action of pulling hair as relief. Obviously, this inflicting behavior over long periods of time can be harmful physically and people who do this eventually look for other escapes by using stress balls or even punching bags.

Below are some more following examples of indicative body language expressions:

Perch lips A.K.A "Fish lips" - Perched lips is a very interesting form of body language, besides having resemblances to a fish's natural expression, this type of body language usually indicates two things. Either disagreement with something said in conversation or perhaps you are thinking of an alternative option that hasn't otherwise been disclosed.

Protecting the Neck or Covering Mouth – This is another intriguing behaviour that occurs sub-consciously and can be traced back to our ancestors from ancient times. Imagine you are at work and a troublesome co-worker who got fired a week ago decides to come back on property and you see him through the window. Your first reaction is to quickly put one hand on your neck or cover your mouth out of shock. In ancient times our ancestors observe beasts such as lions, tigers, and leopards, kill prey in a ferocious manner and the first thing they go for is the neck! So, from a sub-conscious level from thousands of years of evolution our body's first reaction to shock is to quickly cover and protect the neck anytime there is perceived imminent danger present.

Rubbing hands together - People under stress or anxiety tend to rub there hands together in a quick fashion. And if you find that their fingers are interlaced this usually means it's a serious issue that the person is dealing with and is most likely deep in thought.

Sideways head tilt – The sideways head tilt is a sign that your open and receptive to the person or child your engaging. Parents and children both use this form of non verbal communication. Think about it have you ever seen parents, especially mothers raise their children talking to them like drill sergeants with there heads straight and bent down in a condescending manner that connotes dominance? Probably not! -unless they were angry. But instead open and welcoming body language is used by utilizing the sideway head tilt and this action tells children or the person your doing it too they can be at ease and put their guard down.

Direction of Feet – Feet are probably one of the best non-verbal communication indicators that humans use and its hard to mask your true intentions when people analyze your feet. For instance, you're in conversation with someone and although the person is smiling to save face and entertains your banter due to social conventions, his feet start pointing in the opposite direction towards the exit. What does this mean? Although above waist it appears all is fine, but at a closer glance and by observing the direction of his feet you can see where his true motives lie. He doesn't want to continue to talk to you! – But wants to leave as soon as possible and only entertained conversation to be polite.

Common Misconceptions When Reading Body Language

I've already mentioned that when reading body language, you must always keep the context of situation in mind. Popular to contrary belief having your arms crossed does not always mean your reserved or indifferent to others. This is some fluff nonsense pseudoscience that has penetrated mainstream media and is taught in colleges as if it's a fact of life. Although there are definitely situations where folded arms can mean someone is closed off and indifferent towards you, but that is not the case with the majority of people who do this.

In social settings such as parties I've observed people merrily talking to each other with there arms crossed. If we take a closer examination at this behavior one can see that this does not have a negative connotation to it, however it displays self-comfort and not indifference. This is basically a self-hug and a comfortable posture for people to be in. However, if the situation is different and perhaps facial expressions reveal bent eye brows and squinted eyes in conjunction with crossed arms than this person is most likely indifferent and closed off to you.

We are living in a time where technology has enhanced our ability to communicate with one another on a whole different level. We can now send emails and text messages which is a form of communication, but one thing is certain, and I can tell you that a text message will never replace a hug or any other gesture of affection. Despite how advanced our technology is and the amount of high-tech sophistication we posses through telecommunication, we will never be able to replace the value of natural body language. Although its true one can add playful emojis and use punctuation to enhance a text message, but the information provided pales in comparison to a person smiling or crying because in person body language is what can tell you the entire story.

Single finger Pointing Vs Full Palm

Let's face it nobody likes to be pointed at as this non verbal communication is associated with being singled out, outcasted, exiled, punishment and judgement! In ancient times when tribal trial proceedings were passed by the person in ruling authority he would "point" and declare judgement. Thus, pointing connotes this labeling action that promotes some type of punishment. Also, pointing at someone from a psychological stance is kind of like a "sniper shot" and what I mean by this is your specifically singling that individual out which can make that person feel alone and vulnerable. The old adage is true "misery loves company", and studies have shown people tend to cope better in unfavorable situations as long as they have someone with them in similar circumstances.

Nobody wants to be alone. This kind of goes into companionship, loneliness, fulfilment and purpose but I'll get into those subject matters later in the book. On the flipside the full palm point is where you extend all five fingers to point at someone and this is socially acceptable. Have you've ever been at the opera house or watched some sort of performance? The MC almost always introduces the performers with the full palm point, and never does the single finger index point

Chapter 2: Theories of Human Psychology

In this section of the book I'd like to dedicate the subject matter to various theories that encompass identity, social influence, and other complex psychological themes. I want to give you a wide array of psychological perspectives, so you can have exposure to different view points and formulate your own perception and way of thinking.

Law of Reciprocity - The law of reciprocity is something humans intuitively know, especially in the realm of business this law is constantly at work. But what exactly is the law of reciprocity? The idea based on this psychological theory is that there is some sort of equivalent exchange that goes on between two individuals. If someone offers you to do a favor according to the law of reciprocity you will have some sort of inclination that is deeply psychologically rooted to return the favor either equal to the initial favor granted or greater.

Let's look at a practical example, you're at work and you need to take a day off because of a special occasion, perhaps your significant other's birthday, hence you ask your co-worker if he can cover your shift on that particular day although that is his only off day. After negotiating with him he decides to accept working your shift, and now that your shift is covered your free to take that day off. Now this same co-worker comes back 2 weeks later, keep in mind he's always on time, and never misses a shift before. He decides to ask you if you can cover his shift because he has something important to do, and although the first reaction in your mind is to say no because your extremely busy with the kids and family, you realize you have an obligation to return the favor because he initially covered your shift in your time of need.

Therefore, according to the law of reciprocity you have a deep rooted psychological urge to uphold returning the favor. Now let's dissect both individuals in this scenario, its clear you are returning the favor because your co-worker helped you out in your time of need, thus your have a sense of obligation to return the favor. Now let's look at the co-worker, you noticed I mentioned he's always on time and never missed a shift in the past, but for some reason two weeks later he decided to take a day off. Now I understand life happens and it could have been something urgent he really needed to do. But, that's besides the point as what I'm trying to get across is your co-worker intuitively knew he could ask you a favor because your obligated to help him, and hence why he didn't ask any other co-worker. Humans intuitively understand the law of equivalent exchange where to obtain, something of equal value must be lost in order to gain something in return.

Social Conformity & Influence

We all participate in some sort of conformity in one way or another in the society we live in. Whether that's dressing a certain way for work, abiding traffic laws, and following other rules or regulations. When we act accordingly in the right environment life appears to be a lot easier, and you don't have to deal with being chastised or ridiculed because of societal norms. Believe it or not most of our social conformity occurs automatically and basically works like mimicry. Social conformity is what we observe in group behavior, for instance when someone laughs at something your natural inclination would be to mimic that behavior because it appears socially acceptable and you don't want to feel left out, even if you don't understand the joke or find it funny. Have you've ever witnessed a flash mob? People who are not privy to the activity before hand mimic the flash mob in order to socially conform and not look out of place.

The basis of social conformity could have various reasons such as respect for authority, fear of being different, rejection and desire for approval. Whichever reason it maybe we know that the influence of social conformity exists today here in the 21st century and manifests in different forms. But being in front of a group doesn't always necessarily mean it's a good thing. There is a term know as social facilitation, which is where some people may perform better in front of a group while others will not, and this is all dependent on if the person feels that having exposure to a group setting reinforces positivity or fear. From this we can deduce the possible reasons behind why a person gives into social conformity, if its out of fear we know in a group setting you won't perform as well, but if its out of wanting to belong you will perform much better because your desire to belong is so strong.

From a historical point of view, we can see the darker side of social conformity that exists from the Nazis, KKK, slave owners, and on a smaller scale the class room bully. How do groups of people dehumanize and treat other individuals with such cruelty? Do we blame these perpetrators of cruelty as individuals or take a closer look at the context of their situation? Thus, we need to deduce if the behavior of people are exhibiting is individualistic or situational in nature. This can be a difficult task to accurately appraise because there are a multitude of factors at play here. The power of a dark situation where someone is influenced by a negative social conformity especially one in authority can easily dictate an individual's choice despite their personality.

On another more practical example, poverty do we attribute this to people's personal disposition being lazy, unproductive and unqualified or do we attribute it to systemic or institutional imbalances. Politicians are aware of this social phenomenon and exploit it to manipulate people to vote for them. I am not here to pick and choose political sides at any end of the spectrum but just giving you some food for thought.

Group Polarization

This social phenomenon arises when we bring our attitudes and beliefs to a group that also has a common ground you relate too. This usually turns into a "us" versus "them" polar dynamic, and the occurrence of group polarization has greatly increased due to globalization, technology and the global out reach via the internet. The internet has changed the world significantly and has made it much easier for people to communicate and magnify their view points from all parts of the industrialized globe. We observe this working for the greater good of humanity and consequently for the degradation of humanity. What do I mean by this? Well, group polarization via the internet can connect racists, bigots, and misogynist alike to carry out their desires. However, on the opposite side of the spectrum group polarization is behind more positive accomplishments such as educational online resources, crowd funding and other charitable causes.

The dangers found in group polarization is when people become confined to their internal ideologies, logic and way of thinking. Therefore, people within certain group polarizations fail to see other perspectives because they are so caught up in their own rigid belief system. Historic accounts of bad decisions based on group polarization have been revealed throughout history from the water gate cover up to the Chernobyl and Fukushima nuclear disaster. The moral of the story is two heads are better than one as long as they're different perspectives and open to new ideas, innovations and concepts.

Does Power Corrupt?

It was *Lord Acton* the historian and moralist who said it eloquently "absolute power corrupts absolutely." But is this the truth? Uncle Ben from the movie Spiderman has his own insights on this subject and he adamantly states "With great power comes great responsibility." This is a very complex subject to tackle in one sitting, but I personally keep one foot in each of these philosophies and firmly believe a profound truth arises from both these perspectives.

Let's start off with *Lord Acton's* philosophy. The framework behind his thinking and probably his personal observations is that no man should have absolute power. He's probably observed in his life time that people in positions of authority abusing others and becoming corrupt to the power they possess. We see this truth manifested in our reality today with corrupt governments, crooked cops, and shady business partners. The fact is people take advantage of others when given situational power over them, and this can be found in every single type of industry you can think of. Sexual harassment in the workplace is usually perpetrated by someone of higher or senior authority, and if we break this down to the most fundamental level, we see a breech of trust and abuse of power!

Now let's take a look at the fictional character Uncle Ben and his wise words, "with great power comes great responsibility", and this is more of a subtle truth but nonetheless is powerfully liberating. His perception of power is not something that will certainly corrupt you, but it depends on the motive of whoever wields the power. Therefore, emphasis is put on your intention before the power itself, and a good argument can be made for this point, for instance, the gun is a tool designed to take life plain and simple but depending on who wields the gun it can be used to carry out evil acts or for good to protect life. This basically boils down to what intention the wielder of the gun has, which in this case represents power. Policemen or policewomen who live to serve and protect clearly uses their power for the greater good of society, however, a robber uses their power for selfish ambition and illicit gain, and potentially harming other innocent people in the process.

I personally believe the truth is a combination of both these philosophies. I certainly believe that no man should possess absolute power and there should always be both safety and contingency measures in place to intervene someone who holds great power if the need ever arises. The human condition is so frail that sometimes people forget that were all mortal beings living here on earth and will inevitably end up in the grave like everyone else, no human is immortal, nor can we transcend the earthly confines we find ourselves in. We are not immune to death and cannot escape its fate. If you're a believer of some sort of religious denomination that believes in life after death, that's different story for another book all together for us to discuss. But for the sake and purpose of this book I will stick to secular psychology strictly.

Cognitive Dissonance

One of the major concepts in psychology invented by *Leon Festinger* who proposes humans' express feelings of friction when our thoughts, beliefs and behaviors clash with each other. Humans don't like discord, but intuitively want to live in harmony. For example, people who smoke are under cognitive dissonance, they are aware smoking causes cancer, however, they choose to continue to smoke although their beliefs don't really support their behavior. There is an inconsistency because there is a contradiction between the smoker's beliefs and behavior. Ergo, cognitive dissonance can be defined as the discomfort of one's experiences from conflicting beliefs and behavior. As a result, people experiencing cognitive dissonance tend to modify their beliefs in order to justify their behavior, for instance, "I know smoking is bad for my health, but I'm young so I have a strong immune system and can recover quicker from all the toxins I am inhaling."

Or another modification could be "I don't smoke a lot anyways, so my health won't be effected as much". The smoker will modify his belief system to justify his actions and create a sense of perceived harmony in his life. There could be multiple modifications to the smoker's cognition and fundamentally what he is doing is bending the truth to suit his interests, which in this case is smoking. This can be a very self-harming behavior if taken to the extreme, and thus the importance to always weighing the present evidence to the reality we live in to make better informed decisions.

Social & Individual Identity

There are many theories behind what shapes our identity from our peers, media, government, friends, families and even religious denominations. Identity is what we define as the essence of our being and is constructed by life's experiences. It's the core of who we are, our whole life's identity is shaped through our everyday collective experiences which constitute a cohesive reality which reflects our life's story. The burning question is what defines you? Once we break down the social constructs of race, ethnicity, and class who are you deep down inside? Obviously, this is something for you to ponder about and it would take time for you to formulate a valid retrospective answer. You don't need to do so now, but this is just something for you to keep in mind.

Often people define themselves by not who they are, but what they do and the actions they take which define their character. It was the freedom fighter Martin Luthor King who said, *"That a man should be judged not by the color of his skin, but the content of his character"*, and these wise words still echo today. Hypothetically if one was to take away your family, friends, and other things that you hold dearly that you truly love, my question is do you lose apart of your identity? The logic is since family, friends, and institutions helped define and shape your character would the absence of these elements negate who you are as a person? Does this make your existence obsolete? Or do these life experiences only serve as a mere shadow and a nostalgic symbol of your past life? I want you to ponder about this.

The world is constantly changing and evolving and much in the same way our identity is fluid and constantly being remoulded, shaped and influenced by the situational context we find ourselves within. Is the person you were 10 years ago the same person you are today? Obviously, a lot happened within a decade and I would assume that you've changed from your past self and have a different perspective on life from back than. Perhaps your political associations have changed, preferences for clothing, style, whom you associate with and even food. The correct appraisal is there are stages in life in which we find identity for those specific periods of time, and since identity is constantly evolving and changing due to your unique experiences within your situational circumstance, then we cannot just paint identity with the broad stroke of the brush because things are not black and white.

Identity is complex and contains various nuances that shape who we are. The 16 year old you is clearly not the same identity of who you are today. It was more or less a past life experience that is collectively apart of your identity, but not to be mistaken with your current identity or self. You've most likely matured and have better clarity and perception of life than you did as a teenager. And as you progress into an elderly age your identity will naturally be transformed in tandem with your life's experiences and surrounding circumstance. You grow wiser not because of the passage of time elapsing, but through putting the knowledge you have gained from experience into practice.

Consciousness

Social identity is an interesting phenomenon that occurs and can be quite complex to grasp. Consciousness is apart of our individual identity which makes us unique, however social identity is when your consciousness conforms to your personal social surroundings, whether that be your school, friends, family, or workplace. Thus, all the mannerisms, habits, and experiences help define our personal consciousness. But the question is if consciousness is truly an individual or social phenomenon? To find the answer to this enigmatic question we need to dig deeper past surface level thinking and artificial constructs.

I would like to give you a scenario to think about. In the past in the feudal era, kings and families of royalty would live lavishly having only the finest clothing, gourmet food, and other luxuries only the wealthy could afford. But on the other hand, we had peasants who worked as farmers that lived in terrible conditions, and on top of that they had to pay unfair taxes to the crown. Now eventually as history shows when groups of people who are mistreated unfairly for extended periods of time, and continue to perpetually live in conditions of poverty, eventually they start a revolt or revolution!

The interesting thing is when we look at how this idea or proposal of a revolution arose from separate individual consciousnesses, we find people arrive at the same ideology without even communicating with each other! Now this is incredible when you think about it because people who have never spoken a word to each other about the revolution all arrive at the same idea that a revolt needs to happen to tip the scale of wealth in their favor. This happens because although they may have not conventionally spoken to each other in a literal sense they all shared the same experiences of hardship, pain and poverty which is why they all arrive at the same conclusion to immobilize and start a revolution. The ideology of liberation for a more equitable society doesn't even need to be verbally communicated because all the farmers have arrived at the same conclusion consciously.

This same phenomenon can be attributed to terrorism to a lesser degree. A malevolent ideology is created usually to attack western civilizations, and individuals who, with no coordination or knowledge of their peer's actions, act as though they are working towards a common goal or purpose. For instance, a teenager here in America gets radicalized in the name of ISIS and decides to suicide bomb his college. Although he has no direct ties to ISIS let alone communication, yet he identifies with the Islamic state's common goal and ISIS takes credit for his actions, and therefore amalgamating this teenager's identity into ISIS. Ergo, we witness the merging of two separate consciousnesses combined from different parts of the world and keep in mind they never spoke to each other, yet they shared the same common goals, which in this case is to cause destruction to western civilization.

Now I don't want to turn this book into a political theme, but it would make sense that combating the malevolent ideology of ISIS is as equally if not more important than fighting them on the ground. Why? Because you can easily take the life of a terrorist, but that won't solve the problem as you take one down and another will rise. You cannot destroy ideology; however, you can replace it. -That's some food for thought for you to think about.

Memory Theory

John Locke an influential philosopher established memory theory where he states that identity is really a manifestation of collective memories. His logic is your identity exists and retains itself over time because you remember memories of yourself at different points in time of your life, and each of these memories are interconnected to each other from previous ones. His theory parallels experiential theory which states that identity constitutes collective experiences in your life, however according to experiential philosophy your identity is fluid and based on experiential changes collectively, which dictate your identity as a whole.

Obviously in memory theory we don't naturally remember every single detailed account in our lives, however we do remember the significant moments which create chain like memories that are associated to each other. For example, if you remember your first day of school according to memory theory you maintain a memory link to that association. Since you can recall that memory than it is apart of your being, but the issue with memory theory is that nobody remembers from a personal point of view the day of their birth. Do you remember coming out of your mother's womb and all the details surrounding it? Obviously not, thus only certain aspects of this theory are valid while others are incongruent.

Seduction Theory & Experiment

Seduction is an interesting topic to discuss, and there are many social theories on this subject matter. However, I want to talk about one theory and experiment which may interest you. An experiment conducted by a university which recruited young adults to go on a date, however there were a few conditions they had to meet. There were two groups, group(A) and group (B), each group had their own special conditions to follow while on their dates. Group (A) was instructed to disagree with everything they're date brought up, so, for instance if the date liked any particular foods, restaurants, music or any other subject matter group (A) participants would completely disagree and say the opposite of what the date stated.

Now the end result is quite obvious as their dates didn't find this anti-social behavior attractive. You could have probably guessed this already, however, where things get interesting is with group (B) participants who were instructed to disagree only for the first half of the date, and than take a complete 180 degree turn and start being congruent with their dates. The outcome was quite remarkable as dates found all participants in group (B)'s experiment more attractive! Psychologist have many theories behind why this combination of incongruence and congruency creates attraction, but my take on this is that the dates became attracted to group (B) participants because they felt as if they had some sort of impact or "broke through the brick wall" experience.

Now its this impact factor or connection ability whatever you want to call it is what created this seduction and illusion of attraction. When people feel like they impacted or made a difference in someone's life they are more inclined to have a sense of meaning or interest because of their contributing efforts. When it comes to dating there are 3 main factors attention, interest and maintenance. It has ben theorized that an entire life long relationship shifts through these 3 phases attention, interest and maintenance in order to sustain longevity. Think about it let's say you meet your significant other at college or a bar and you manage to capture his or her attention. From there you need to create interest in order to attract your potential mate, and than lastly comes commitment which is the long term maintenance phase. However, if you just stay stuck in commitment phase without cycling back to attention or interest you may not end up in a long term relationship because you neglected the other two cycles.

Do humans only need commitment to sustain a long term relationship? Or are there other factors involved like cycling through the 3 phases to sustain a relationship to keep each spouse happy? We all have that friend or know that person where we think "wow, this is such an amazing person I wonder why he or she has trouble finding someone?" Perhaps this individual is really good at the maintenance phase but is not so good at attention or interest. This is definitely worth thinking about.

Understanding Anxiety

Everybody struggles with some level of anxiety, but the intensity varies from person to person. Contrary to popular belief anxiety can be a good thing, and in other cases determinantal to a person's health. Imagine you have an upcoming exam and this test will determine 60% of your grade you would probably become anxious, however this anxiety is what will fuel your motivation to study all day for the upcoming exam. Where anxiety becomes harmful is when it is irrational and promotes no positive working habits. By measuring the outcome of your anxiety, you can determine if its anxiety that connotes positive or negative effects. The fear of failing the test and potentially creating an obstacle for your future educational pathway is what positive anxiety reinforces by making you study, so you can successfully pass your examination. Whereas if anxiety creates a crippling or debilitating effect to the point where you cannot do anything constructive and stay confined in your fears living out your personal limiting belief systems or self-fulfilling prophesies of failure is when you know your anxiety is getting out of hand.

In the modern world everyone is going to have anxiety for different reasons. Perhaps you have a little anxiety to be punctual for work, so your boss doesn't chastise you and ultimately you can retain long term employment. Again, we see a positive anxiety reinforcing you to mobilize yourself to take action towards getting to work on time, hence avoiding any disciplinary actions or even worse termination. Imagine if you had a carefree attitude towards being punctual to work? -This wouldn't sit well with your employer, and thus you would quickly end up in the unemployment line by not having a healthy dose of perceived fear.

The notion of completely eliminating anxiety is erroneous and misunderstood. Anxiety can enhance performance and helps us stay on our toes, thus making us more self-aware, sharp, and just gives us better overall mental acumen over our circumstances. If you actually think about it the absolute absence of anxiety could potentially lead to psychopathy! As psychopaths have no anxiety or perceived fear.

So, what about people who struggle with anxiety disorders? The thing is people who have had anxiety disorders have been exposed to negative unresolved anxieties for extended periods of times. They tend to have a history of anxious bouts since childhood and later develop into debilitating fears or anxiety attacks which effects their personal lives. Anxiety can occur at any point in our life at different ages, and there is an interesting phenomenon with people in there early 30s being diagnosed with onset of general anxiety when they had no previous history of anxious bouts. But why is this?

With closer examination we can see that usually when people hit their 30s that's when life begins, they start families, have kids, house mortgages and have to pay bills. Its no longer the carefree days of your 20s where you looked forward getting drunk on the weekend, party all night, and live with minimal responsibilities. Now you have more pressing and important matters to deal with and huge responsibilities, thus it makes sense why people who are unprepared for adulthood get diagnosed with general anxiety disorders later on in life yet have no past history of anxious bouts.

Anxiety can take place in many forms from social anxiety, phobias (fear of heights, insects), and avoidance. Each of these disorders' common denominator is triggered by anxiety or fear, where fear is disproportionate to the stimulus. These labels are not designed to create stigmas for people to have a noose tied around their necks for the rest of their lives, but these labels serve as markers that identify the specific state of anxiety you struggle with and are diagnostic tools to use to help implement a solution that is designed to work for you.

Triggers of Anxiety Disorders

The cause of anxiety has many pathways and can be traced back to a variety of reasons depending on each situation. There could be certain physiological aspects that make you more susceptible to anxiety disorders like neurotransmitter imbalances or hereditary factors. But overall anxiety disorders are a psychological problem that is misinterpretation of the reality the person suffering from lives within. How we attribute or ascribe meaning to certain scenarios and outcomes can determine the surfacing of anxiety or the level of intensity it holds. For example, you call or text a friend and you don't get a response from her for over 5 hours and you attribute her unresponsiveness to the message you sent her and start thinking you did something wrong, and thus you elicit anxiety within yourself psychologically because of all these chain thoughts that triggered it.

But at a closer glance of the situation your friend was probably busy doing something important hence why she refrained from messaging you. Therefore, case in point that anxiety can be a misinterpretation of the reality you live in when you attribute a skewed interpretation for a particular circumstance. Anxiety can come from anywhere from overprotective parents, societal standards, social norms, and bullying. Ergo, when we are looking at the origins of anxiety, we need to look at the whole picture to understand the nature of anxiety disorders, from personal experiences, culture, physiological disposition, and learnt anxiety.

General Physiological & Psychological signs of anxiety:

Heart pulse racing

Dizzy

Sweaty palms

Headaches

Perpetually perceived negative experiences

Difficulty focusing

Avoidance

Jitteriness

Pupils dilated

Fiddling with hands

Restless leg syndrome

Hyper-vigilance

*The above listed symptoms are hallmark signs indicative of anxiety.

Controlling Anxiety Through Stress Management

The truth is anxiety cannot be prevented, but it can be controlled through stress management strategies. The nature of anxiety is dynamic and is influenced by many external stimuli that affect each person differently. So, what are things you can do to manage your anxiety? You can exercise, get adequate sleep, eat healthy, developing rituals or routines, create positive social relations, and being self-aware of how you think. One of the key components to managing anxiety is being mindful of your thought process on a sub-conscious level, how do you talk to yourself or refer to yourself as? Do you have accumulated negative thoughts about yourself or an inferiority complex? Catch yourself thinking these detrimental thoughts and recognize that these are harmful and replace them with more positive reinforcing thoughts.

Something as simply giving yourself a positive vocabulary during self-talk can be a big aid for you when dealing with anxiety and the many stresses it entails.

Remember anxiety can be mentally draining causing you to allocate all your attention and mental energies into places that don't need them, and as a result neglecting other essential areas of your personal life making you perform poorly, such as school, work, and among friends.

How to Recognize if Your Significant Other Is Socially Anxious

How can we identify the tell tale signs of social anxiety among your spouse? There are a few anxious signs your significant other may give off such as avoiding social functions like family get togethers, workplace events, and any other social gatherings. Your spouse may be a wonderful experience 1 on 1 but may choke in a social setting, hence their avoidance of being around other people. The reason for this could be because your significant other must do a work presentation or public speaking gig, and you may notice more jitteriness, or they may have trouble sleeping. Ultimately, remember its you spouse's perception of being judged negatively by others which triggers social anxiety, and their primary concern is being evaluated by the people around them.

There is a misconception that people who have social anxiety are socially awkward, but this is not the case as people with social anxiety just don't perform as well or not as comfortable in a public setting as oppose to a more close, confined and intimate one. This is why ever since the advent of online dating, we see people with social anxiety performing extremely well because they are able to hide behind a keyboard or smart-phone when communicating to their potential new mate.

Chapter 3: Instantly Read People

Cold Reading Vs Comprehensive Reading

Curiosity is a critical component to aid you in reading people more comprehensively. Cold reading occurs by observing non verbal communication and looking for cues where you can draw some conclusions or assumptions. Cold reading encompasses your day to day interaction with people on a more shallow surface level, such as the subway. Imagine your in the subway you see people from all walks of life dressed uniquely, listening to music, reading the newspaper, and even potentially observing others just like you.

The truth is cold reading can only go so far in regard to analyzing people. You may be able to pick up some interesting body language, perhaps the person is slouched while sitting which indicates lethargic tendencies, exhibiting pensiveness or anxiety through "restless leg syndrome", looking at a mirror to cover up blemishes shows insecurity, and perhaps wearing a lot of jewelry which displays vanity. With these clues you can formulate some sort of speculation on the person's current state of being and personality, however you cannot really uncover who they are as a person and their motives with a superficial cold read.

This is where curiosity comes into play. In order to get more information about someone simply observing and monitoring their behavior can only go so far and gives you a one dimension perspective of the entire picture. Thus, you need to have a certain level of engagement by utilizing curiosity and ask the 4 fundamental questions *who, what, where and why*. There was a social experiment conducted by two people and they approached this rugged, unshaved, torn clothed homeless man who had the strong scent of alcohol on him, and gave him $50 bucks.

The natural assumption based on a quick cold read was that he would probably use most if not all the cash on more alcohol to drown out his misery and find some form of escape from his plight. However, despite the tell tale signs of an alcoholic when he was followed by these two social scientists they were astonished when they discovered he didn't use a dime on alcohol, but on the contrary he went to the grocery store and bought non perishable food items and distributed rations to some of his other homeless friends. This scenario shows you why cold reading is not always accurate, although you can use it as a quick gauge and instant assessment on an individual based on non-verbal communication, however you cannot arrive at a definitive conclusion.

The example I discussed shows all the tell tale signs of an alcoholic justifying the deductive reasoning that this homeless man would most likely buy more alcohol, but instead did something completely unexpected. This is why curiosity through answering the 4 fundamental questions is how you want to comprehensively analyze someone to grasp the entire situation.

Deductive Reasoning

We've all seen *Sherlock Holmes* solve the most puzzling and gruesome mysteries by simply putting all the facts together in a coherent manner. The method he employs is known as deductive reasoning, which is basically the art of reasoning backwards, determining a cause from an observable effect. There are other factors that need to fall into place in order to successfully use deductive reasoning effectively.

Criteria:

1. ***Observe Behavior*-** The first thing on the list you need to look for in order to carry out deductive reasoning appropriately is to observe a person's behavior from their demeanor, other hallmark traits, and their M.O also known as mode of operation. (modus operandi) Your looking for their work habits or behavior in each situation or context.

2. ***Process of Elimination*** – This is what I call a filter tactic that helps you sift out speculations you may arrive at that are not backed by your personal observations and facts. Sherlock Holmes once said, *"Once you eliminate the impossible, whatever remains, however improbable must be the truth."* In the end only one truth will prevail and arise from your many conjectures, and its this truth that remains after you have eliminated all your flawed speculations.

What your trying to do in essence is filter out all possible assumptions based on the available evidence you have present. I'll give you a scenario, you see someone who appears extremely sleep deprived, you observe an introverted demeanor and school bag present. You have two theories either this person was up late night partying or studying, and you eliminate one of these speculative assertions by weighing it against the evidence. In this case the two points of evidence you have present is his demeanor which is subjective to your perception and more concrete objective evidence his school bag which is indicative of someone who attends some form of school or institution.

Based on these merits we can eliminate the assumption of this individual partying, since his demeanor appears to be one of an introvert and he posses an object that we ascribe to students. Ergo, as Sherlock Holmes stated, "whatever remains, however improbable must be the truth". In this case its not really something we would consider improbable, but more the likely option which is this person was up late night studying. This was a more simplistic example of how the process of elimination works, but you get the gist of it now.

3. ***The Rule of Thumb*** - The standard rule of thumb when using deductive reasoning is ensure you have enough information or data present on your person in question. Often the available evidence may be sparse, and not vast enough to enable you to make a definitive conclusion. Most the time we narrow down our reasoning to 2-3 theories and this is completely fine as its better to have multiple speculations than a baseless assumption that you propose as the truth.

Also, to add to this rule of thumb never speculate without data! Sherlock Holmes said, "It's a capital mistake to theorize before one has data, inevitably one twists facts to suit theories rather than theories to suit facts." This is a common mistake made by people of the general public because they jump to conclusions without assessing the full context of the situation and allow their soiled perceptions of the facts dictate their theories.

Therefore, if there isn't enough information to solve a problem or analyze someone. You need to do more reconnaissance and collect more intel in order to arrive at a reasonable conclusion.

4. **Structure** – Deductive reasoning should be structured, organized, and flow coherently in order to be used effectively. Without a clear objective in sight, it can be hard to focus on where exactly your end result may be. Thus, the importance of establishing structure which creates a clear objective that allows our mind to consciously focus on managing our mental energies and allocating these resources to solving the problem at hand. This is where the fundamental 4 questions come into play who, what, where and why? For instance a simple question may be what is this person's occupation?

5. **Do Not Neglect The Obvious** - No matter how convoluted a person may be to read or how complicated a problem is do not neglect the simple faculties that can help you evaluate the situation successfully. Its always the core principles that will be the mechanisms that help you deduce even the most mysterious people.

6. **Visualization** - Visualization makes you become more self-aware. Visualizing actions before you perform them sharpens your mind, hones analytical prowess, and raises your awareness level. You become more mindful of the context you find yourself in the more you practice visualization, and this shows you how much you really know about your surroundings. Thereby, enabling you to be more meticulous when you are acting on your plans.

7. **Discuss Your Findings With Others (optional)** – This is an optional step to deductive reasoning but enhances its efficacy. Having two minds is better than one, thus being able to assert your theories and describe them to someone else will help allow you to get another perspective and potential feedback of the inconsistencies and possible holes in your speculation. You get your own

perspective analyzed by someone else who holds his or her own unique take of the situation, whether you agree or not doesn't matter the point is being able to here someone else's side and weighing it against your own take. Again, this is completely optional but if you do have the option to have someone to talk to when your analyzing somebody, I would encourage you to participate in discussing your findings. Remember sometimes people have the uncanny ability to stimulate epiphany moments in you unintentionally.

Mindset Strategies

In order to hone your analytical skills to your full potential you need to understand a few elements before starting out. Below are 3 mindset strategies you need to incorporate for you to get the most out of deductive reasoning.

Deep Level Observations – Deep observations go beyond surface level glances but instead try to establish cause and effect rationale with whatever information is gathered. Remember if you do not have enough intel to go on to fit the pieces of the puzzle together, then I strongly urge you to collect more information, so you do not end up forcing the puzzle pieces to fit and making the facts suit the theories.

So, in theory deep level observation sounds great but how can I put this into practice? Simply start making conscious efforts to be actively engaged in your conversations with people, be cognizant of the finer details from micro-expressions, abnormal body language and situational context. Do not have your attention divided or focus distracted try your best to be present minded and observe your environment.

Be Skeptical – The renaissance arguably one of the greatest periods of time in human history where humanity reached enlightenment and started making some serious advancements in both science and technology. One of the primary guiding principles of this time that we still use today is being "skeptical". Basing things on empirical evidence which means observable things with cause and effect that can be proved again and again repeatedly. We no longer had to abide by oldwives tales and myths that constructed our perception of the world we live in.

Thus, when your trying to read someone remember to always bring a healthy dose of skepticism that will remove your personal biases which may influence your inferences. Take the facts and weigh them against the reality you've experienced and background knowledge.

Statistical Probability - You need to think like a scientist! When analyzing people, you need to be realistic and think in terms of probability meaning what is most likely going to occur. Forming hypothesises as you go along and testing them as you gather new data. After producing many hypothesises than you use the process of elimination by eliminating your most unlikely speculations. Technically speaking using probability to analyze people is considered inductive reasoning because deductive reasoning uses certainty and sound logic to form an answer, but inductive reasoning uses the framework of what is the most likely answer given the facts.

Most problems in life you come across never gives you all the information necessary, thus you tend to have missing pieces of information. Hence, using inductive reasoning too is something you should become accustom with.

Observing Vs Looking

What is the difference between observing and looking? When we quickly glance at something without truly being aware of what were glancing at, we are engaged in looking behavior. But when we observe someone, or something how does this differ? Observing is essentially monitoring people under your two lenses taking notes and being aware of the information your sensory detectors or organs (your eyes) is receiving. Ultimately being able to have an outcome derived by capturing a sight of an object and this is fundamentally the difference between looking and observing. With looking visual information is coming in and out without a thought but observing has you processing the visual information coming in and out and being able to arrive at a conclusion from what you've observed.

Listening Vs Hearing

Listening and hearing are two terms that often are mistakenly used in the same text as if they're interchangeable, however this is not the case as these two terms hold two completely different meanings. Hearing is simply using your sensory or auditory ability to perceive sound which naturally occurs passively. Listening on the other hand is making a conscious decision to perceive sound and allow your brain to decipher meaning from the words and sentences that are being spoken to you.

Facial Profiling

Technically speaking, facial profiling can be defined as the tendency to photograph a human face, or to scan it, so that you can use the image to identify someone according to the unique characteristics of their face. Government departments find this process useful for the purpose of identifying criminals.

In general, however, facial profiling is the use of one's facial features to analyze the person as a whole; including the person's personality, feelings, intentions, and so on. It is easy to appreciate the importance of facial features if you imagine being presented with a blank face – not blank just without expressions, but literally blank without the varying physical features. You would not have a clue what kind of person that face belonged to.

On the contrary, a face with a pointed nose or raised eyebrows may give you helpful ideas about the person to whom the face belongs, and your opinion is likely to be quite different from the one you formed when you look at a face with short nose and probably squinting eyes.

Facial Movements

However, the physical appearance is not all there is to facial profiling. Suppose, for instance, you are looking at a painting of someone with a broad smile. Would that make you conclude the person is happy? Probably, yes. But you may not necessarily be right. You need to study facial movements to be able to tell with near accuracy what the person's feelings are. Or have you not seen people smiling with bitterness; a smile full of spite?

A good example of how inconclusive a static facial picture can be is the historic *Mona Lisa* of the legendary painter, Leonardo da Vinci. Some people have interpreted the enigmatic smile portrayed in the 16th century painting to be friendly and warm, others have seen shrewdness in it, and many others have given an incredibly vast range of interpretations. The question is: What would make different people come to a similar, or at least, near close, conclusion? It is movement of facial muscles.

If you watch someone smile, probably as they speak, or as they listen to someone else speak, you may notice that there are some parts of the face that move in a certain manner, which may inform you of the emotions accompanying the smile. A smile that is flashed just to be polite is accompanied by muscle movements that are different from those that accompany a genuine smile of joy. Even a smile reflecting cynicism is unique and unlike other types of smiles.

In short, body movement and emotions relate to transmit information within the context of socio-emotional communication. In this regard, it is possible to extract information from people by studying their facial expressions, body movements, and the shifting of their eye gaze. It is the information you gather in this manner that you rely on to deduce a person's thought process, mood, and even intention. The whole process from observing people and perceiving related information is what enables social interaction. Otherwise it would be extremely difficult for people to relate with one another if there was no way of 'reading' another person.

Animals In The Wild Read Body Language Too!

Human beings are not alone at benefitting from facial profiling. Other social animals, such as bees and ants also benefit from it. How is that possible, you may wonder? Well, by observing certain familiar facial features, the animals can tell which animal belongs to their own species and which one does not. This helps them in matters of security among other things. In fact, bees, wasps and ants are among social insects that can even distinguish those that belong to the same nest as themselves and those that do not.

Therefore, facial profiling should not appear strange or so much out of the normal when it comes to human beings, considering people are intelligent animals who can learn what to look for in facial profiling in addition to the natural talents one is born with. If a paper wasp, as it were, can recognize another individual, not just identifying other paper wasps as a species, how much more can a human being do? In fact, paper wasps are quite good at face discrimination, where they can read varying facial features of one insect as distinct from another.

Instantly Read People's Motives

One of the important things facial profiling helps you achieve is to understand what motive a person has. If the motive is noble, you will be at ease, and if it has malice, you will take precautionary measures. Depending on the situation, this kind of understanding can mean the difference between career success and failure, business success and failure, or even life and death.

Still, for you to be proficient at facial profiling, you need to put what you learn into practice, and sometimes it will appear like a trial and error method. However, once you have mastered the skills, you will be adept at distinguishing trustworthy people from pretenders, dangerous people from those who are safe to be around and so on. At the same time, you will cease to take people's actions at face value, but instead evaluate actions with the person's motive in mind. To be on track with face profiling, you need to first understand the real meaning of motive and the real meaning of behavior.

Behavior is a variety of actions that go hand in hand with certain mannerisms. Behavior is observable and detectable as you just need to see, hear or feel the other person act. If someone hits another one on the arm, you will have observed the person's behavior. However, you may not be in a position to tell whether the action was done in good faith or in malice, unless you know the motive for the person hitting the other.

At face value, hitting someone else appears to be a bad action. However, suppose the person hit the other on the arm in a bid to smash a dangerous insect? Would the person still be judged as malicious? In such instances, the look on the person's face would, very likely, have shown you that the action was being carried out as a protective measure. Probably the feelings of worry and concern for the other person would be written all over the face of the person doing the hitting.

A motive is the reason behind someone's action. In fact, motive precedes behavior. For example, when students cheat in an exam, it is often because they want to impress someone. It might be their subject teachers that they want to impress, their parents, or even their friends. Such students will walk with their heads high once the results are out and they have passed with flying colors. However, there could be a student who cheats in an exam to avoid the wrath of an unreasonable or abusive teacher, guardian or classmate. Such a student is unlikely to walk with gait even after passing the exam. While arrogance might be written all over the faces of the first group of students, guilt might be the emotion showing on the face of the latter student.

Such are the interpretations that provide a good guide as to how to handle the perpetrators of bad actions. In short, it is erroneous to take an action at face value, because it can mislead you into making the wrong conclusions.

Does it mean motive is always calculated? Well, it is often calculated, but there are certain actions that you undertake following certain motives that you do not consciously think about. Suppose you are having a meal, for example, why do you chew your food? The reason you chew your food is to ensure it is prepared for swallowing. Yet you do not take time to contemplate how you are going to chew and how smooth you want the food to be. Instead, you carry out your actions unconsciously. How about blocking a blow when someone is about to hit you? It is the same thing. There are some actions that are spontaneous and involuntary, even though they are not without motive.

However, there are times you can observe someone's face and conclude they are consciously thinking about their eating behavior, for instance, when they are trying to get meat off a bone. The way the eyes and the jaws will be moving can be great giveaways.

As a social animal, you are bound to interact with other people on a day-to-day basis. Those people will behave in different ways towards you, and while some of their actions will benefit you, others will put you at a disadvantage whether socially, economically or otherwise. However, by understanding the motives of the people around you, it becomes easy for you to influence their next course of action, or even to act in a way that cushions you from potential damage emanating from those people's actions. And how do you get to know other people's motives? Once again, the secret lies in reading their faces.

In his song, *The Gambler*, Kenny Roger's fellow gambler tells him he has made his life reading people's faces. He could tell the cards the people held in their hands even if the cards were hidden from him, just by observing the look on the holder's face. This is what facial profiling is about. In this case, Roger's pal was often able to pull a brilliant gambling move by reading the face of his opponent.

Along similar lines, Donald Trump, in his book, *The Art of the Deal*, speaks of the importance of understanding the other person's motive. If the person's facial look and general behavior portray desperation, Trump is able to take advantage of the situation to get himself a better business deal. A good example would be where someone is trying to sell property in order to repay pressing debts. The look on the face of such a person would, in the depth of the negotiations, show emotions that are different from those shown by another person trying to sell similar property to raise money for charity.

In short, it is imperative that you understand the motives of the people around you if you are to relate with them in a way that makes you comfortable and successful. After all, the motives of people with whom you associate have a way of affecting your well being, your finances, and other different aspects of your life.

If you can decipher the motives and realize they are beneficial to you, then you can behave in a manner that encourages the other person to continue doing whatever it is the person is doing. On the other hand, if, when you decipher the motives, you realize they are bad for you, the realization gives you opportunity to behave in a manner that discourages or deters the other person from proceeding with the intended action. Alternatively, it can prompt you to behave in a way that mitigates the damage caused by the person's action.

It is important to learn the skills of facial profiling because people do not normally freely portray the motives behind their actions. While in cases of speech you would be advised to read between the lines, in the case of actions, the best thing you can do is to read the person's face so you can deduce the emotions responsible for prompting the actions. Just as a reputable businessperson keenly tries to decipher the emotions of the opponent in order to know how best to influence the deal to his or her own advantage, you need to decipher the emotions behind anyone you are dealing with socially and otherwise for your own sake.

Another important reason why you need to hone the skills that can help you decipher people's motives is ability to deflect aggression. People do not always portray negative behavior towards you because they despise you as a person. Sometimes they can even manifest aggression towards you just because they believe you are eyeing the same promotion that they are. If you detect such competition as the motive, you may be able to allay the person's fears. That may not necessarily call for your backing off from contention, but you might decide to be more tactful. In short, understanding the motive behind the behavior of someone with whom you associate can put you at a tactical advantage when designing your response.

How Non Verbal Communication Influences Facial Profiling?

While the term facial profiling invokes the idea of someone's character based on how the person's facial features look like, the reality is that the best way to understand someone is in context. Whether the person is speaking verbally or just responding silently to what is being said by people around them, it is easy to understand the person's real attitude when you understand the environment they are in.

If, for instance, you were meant to meet some friends at a restaurant for dinner, and you ended up running late but eventually turned up one hour late, you might have apologized on arrival and expressed your concern that you thought they might have begun without you. Suppose one of them responded in a cool voice: Our plan was to wait for you till tomorrow morning.

While such a statement could be taken as normal in a situation where a group of friends had gone out on an adventure, it certainly cannot be normal where friends had planned to have dinner together at a restaurant. Of course, in the dinner date situation everyone at table must have understood the statement to be sarcastic because they knew the whole picture; the circumstances and environment within which the statement was said. In short, understanding the environment surrounding a given piece of verbal communication helps to extract the correct message.

By this explanation, we are underlining the importance of trying to understand other factors that help to understand people and their communication, besides the words they use. People often think they can learn a lot about a person from their verbal communication, but the truth is that it is very easy for someone to manipulate you as an observer with what they say. As such, verbal communication on its own may not paint a true picture of what the person's attitude and feelings are. A good example is when people choose to be sarcastic as in the example cited above.

There is no sphere of life where attention is not required for a person to succeed. In class, for example, you need to pay attention to the teacher if you are to understand what is being taught, and to your classmates if you are to be a productive participant in a group project. You also require similar attention, because for the teacher to respond appropriately to your question he or she must listen carefully to your question and concerns.

That scenario is replicated in other areas of life, including sales, where salespeople and potential customers must pay attention to one another in order to succeed each in their own interest. In sales, there are times the sales representative impresses the potential customer within the first two minutes. In cases where such salespeople do not quickly pick up the vibe that they have already won their potential customers, there is the danger of continuing to give their standard sales pitch non-stop.

In this fast modern world, people have a thousand and one things to do in a day, and if you are the type of salesperson who cannot read facial expressions and other para-verbal communication, your potential clients are likely to bid you goodbye with a request that you give them a call in future. So, how could such a salesperson have detected that he had won the client already? Well, this is easy. When someone is paying attention, it means you are saying something they like, and the minute such a person stops paying attention, it means they have heard enough. For your benefit, you need to translate such cessation of attention to mean it is time for you to give that person room to respond.

The problem is that some salespeople do not even realize when their potential client is paying attention, and so a good part of their talk is geared towards trying to make the person pay attention. Without a doubt, such lack of understanding is disastrous in business. If you want to know if a person is paying attention to you, observe if the person is:

1. Maintaining eye contact

You can tell that a person is paying attention when their whole face is directed to your side, and the person is actually looking at you but not staring. Such a person is likely to have the trunk of the body leaning a little forward, showing they are open to hearing more from you. The message you should read from someone in this position is that they are fully present and paying attention to you.

2. Smiling

A warm smile communicates that the other person is listening and paying full attention to you. It also gives the message that you are speaking to the right person. To use the same example of a salesperson trying to win a potential customer, you are unlikely to begin second guessing yourself wondering if you are targeting the wrong people, if the person you are speaking to is warm and receptive.

3. Relaxed

If the person you are speaking to is relaxed, meaning they do not have their arms or legs crossed as they look at you, they are likely to be perceptive to what you are saying. If they are truly relaxed, they will also not be shifting in their seat, appear agitated nor will they have their hands in their pockets. And, of course, they will have their whole body facing in your direction.

4. Questioning

When a person seeks clarity in the middle of your presentation, it means the person is paying attention to what you are saying, and they are not listening out of sheer politeness. You can also learn a lot from their facial mannerisms as they speak to you.

How to Read Micro-expressions

First of all, it is important to understand that micro-expressions are not the same as the normal look that a person consciously wears, for example, during an interview or during a conference. Micro-expressions are more involuntary than intentional. In fact, for the most part, people only realize later that they made certain expressions, and sometimes they do not even realize it, because it is not deliberate. It follows that for you as an observer to pick up such micro-expressions and make good use of them, you need to be attentive and have the skills to decipher the meaning of each of those tiny expressions.

-The Commonest Micro-expressions as explained by Dr. Ekman

The seven universally acknowledged micro-expressions of a person are happiness, fear, disgust, contempt, anger, surprise and sadness. A micro-expression occurs so fast that unless an observer is keen it is easy to miss it. It actually lasts between a fifteenth and a twenty-fifth of a second. Dr. Paul Ekman who has done extensive research on how to decode the human face has been able to prove that facial micro-expressions are universal. In short, even if you are from the northern hemisphere, if you are sad there are some micro-expressions that will automatically show on your face that are similar to someone from the southern hemisphere with the same experience as yourself.

This expert, who inspired the show, 'Lie to Me', has proven that even people who were born blind, and hence have not seen other people's facial expressions, display the same micro-expressions as everyone else. This goes on to confirm that although people who share different cultures and environments also share some common traits, micro-expressions are not necessarily tied to one's background or environment. Rather, they are natural and biological as proven by the fact that congenitally blind people express the same micro-expressions for basic emotions as people who can see normally.

It is important to understand how to interpret the micro-expressions in order to understand the people we associate with in our daily lives. After learning the emotion represented by each expression, it is a good idea to try expressing it before a mirror, so that you can correlate the feelings and facial expression better. After all, it has been established that although a person's feelings trigger specific facial expressions, an expression can itself trigger a specific emotion. In short, the emotion-expression relationship is two-way, working directly and conversely.

What this, essentially, means is that if you create a facial expression of sadness and let it remain for a while, soon you will be feeling sad. On the other hand, if you decide to smile at people in a gathering even before they have said anything to affect your emotions, soon you will be experiencing joy.

Often when a person's face develops significant horizontal wrinkles, it is a sign that the person is contemplating something, and when the wrinkles appear vertically between the eyebrows, it shows the person's high level of concentration.

Guide Lines For Facial Profiling

1) Always have a baseline

Individuals have certain behavior patterns and idiosyncrasies, and it always helps your facial profiling exercise when you know what those are. There are some people, for example, who will never look at you in the eye whether you are awarding them a medal or admonishing them. To them, social life goes on without looking people in the eye, and that is them – the character that forms them under normal circumstances.

When it comes to the skills of facial profiling, one of the telltale signs of someone who has something to hide is avoiding eye contact. However, if you have this behavior as your target person's baseline, there is no way you are going to rely on it to help you catch the culprit of wrongdoing. On the other hand, if you were interviewing someone for a post requiring someone who can ask candid questions, you are not going to dismiss this kind of person.

In short, certain mannerisms and forms of body language normally included in facial profiling should be dismissed or relegated to the backburner if they form your target person's baseline. When studying someone, it is best to be objective of that person's normal behavior, so that you do not read deception where there is none, evasiveness and guilt where none exists and so on.

2) Identify deviations

The deviations you need to be looking for are those behaviors that do not conform to normal behavior even after factoring in the individual's unique mannerisms. If someone who rarely looks up when talking faces you with a stone face when talking to you, this should raise questions. This behavior must be deliberately displayed, which means the person is sharp enough to understand that looking down is likely to indicate evasiveness.

In short, if someone whose baseline you know behaves contrary to their normal behavior, you need to probe further. There are also times you may know someone's baseline, but you find other body language signs that make you still not trust the person. In the instance where someone is normally known to avoid eye contact, you are certainly not going to use lack of eye contact as a sign the person is culpable. However, if the person keeps tapping the floor with one foot or keeps tapping the knee or moving the hand from the knee to the lap and even to the forehead, you may classify this person as requiring further investigation.

3) Read signs as a cluster

Even after identifying one sign that falls under the telltale signs of, for example, cheaters, it is important to look out for other signs that might back up that one sign you have noticed. In the example cited earlier in the book about someone seated with folded arms on a cold day, the emphasis was on the importance of taking the environment into account.

However, you need not be quick to dismiss the possibility of the person being disinterested in what is going on in the room. The best thing would be to look out for other signs that are manifested by a person not interested in what is being said or done, and if the person you are focused on shows one or more of those signs, then it would be reasonable for you to conclude the person is bored or simply has no interest in the happenings.

4) Compare behavior for Inconsistencies

In case you pick up a clue that this person may fit your criteria, but you either do not have the person's baseline or there are no other body language signs to support that single clue, it is usually a good idea to change tact. This does not mean you cease to use body language clues, but rather you make some alterations to the environment.

One of the best ways to try and see if the person will remain consistent in behavior is by you exiting the scene as you allow someone else or other people to come in and continue with the conversation with your target person. That way, you will all be able to compare notes and see what gestures and body language signs have been consistent and which ones have varied with changing setups.

In fact, if there is opportunity for you to observe the person yourself without the person seeing you peep, the way it happens with formal crime interrogations, you can do your first hand comparisons and see what signs tally and which ones contrast with what you saw when you were near the person.

Do you see the person's facial expressions change or do they remain the same as they were when you were engaging the person? Has the person's posture changed? If the person was held back or sat with arms tightly held together and legs folded back or crossed, and now the person is seated with legs straightened and spread out, and with arms free with probably one hand on the table as the person looks straight at your replacement, you should have a lot more to investigate about this person.

This is because the demeanor of the person when you interacted with him was one of someone who is naturally reserved, but when someone else took your place your target person's demeanor changed to reflect a person who is free and outgoing. This can be translated to mean the person is deliberately creating a particular image for your sake, and, very likely, he wants your interaction with him to end as soon as possible before you start digging into something, he does not want you to know.

5) Read the mirror message

The mirror message presents itself to you the way your image shows up in a mirror in front of you. The only difference is that this time what is reflected is behavior. How this mirror message works is based on the fact that people are likely to reciprocate your behavior with similar behavior. If you approach someone with a smile, chances are they are going to smile back. This happens even when you are approaching total strangers.

This is because there are neurons in the brain that are biologically set to reflect what we translate as going on in other people's mind. You have an internal system that reads other people's body language, and when you have developed a perception towards another person, the image is normally reflected on you. If you are in a group and are keen, you will observe a number of people frown if just one of you makes a pronounced frown the way people do when contemplating something to say. Sometimes it just takes a yawn from one person for the entire group to yawn in a disordered chain.

If with this knowledge you see someone who does not mirror your clear and pronounced behavior in any way, you need to wonder why. For someone to remain stone-faced when you have presented a very warm smile is a cause for concern. Is this person a sadist? Does this person have a grudge against you? Does this person despise you? Is this person unhappy with something you have said or done? In short, if people do not mirror what is biologically normal, then you need to be on the alert as something is not right.

6) Distinguish the strongest voice within a group

When you are trying to communicate to a group of people, it is easy to focus on the group leader, because, in your view, if the leader buys into your idea it is easy for her to influence the rest of the group. Whereas that is basically true, it falls short if the leader happens to have a weak voice.

The point here is that it is possible to have someone else in the group with a stronger voice than the leader, and that is the person you should focus on. In fact, in cases where the leader does not have a strong voice, she usually relies on the sentiments of other people in the group to make a decision, and that is because she or he does not feel confident enough to make a decision on the next course of action. Since, even with an opinion of her own, she is still influenced by those with stronger voices, it is best to win over the person with the strongest voice in the first place. In any case, such a person has the capacity to influence the other members of the group.

The challenge you have is to identify the person with the strongest voice among all, but it becomes easy when you know what traits to look for. A person with a strong voice is confident, and her body language says it. Her voice is strong, and she/he has a big smile. Also, when she/he sits or stands, her/his posture is expansive; meaning she/he does not recoil to herself/himself the way timid or shy people do. Note that a strong voice is different from a loud one, and you should avoid confusing the two. Some people who speak loudly are not necessarily influential among their peers.

7) Manner of walking

You can tell the level of a person's confidence by how they walk. People who shuffle their feet as they walk usually lack in confidence. They may not feel self assured, or they may not be certain about whatever is going on. Another sign that a person lacks in self confidence is if they face down as they walk. On the contrary, a confident person looks straight up and does not hesitate to meet people's eyes.

One way you can help someone who lacks in self confidence is to compliment them on something. There is always something good you can say about someone without it sounding like flattery. Unfortunately, people often think of physical appearance when they think of compliments, but you can also compliment a shy person for punctuality or sheer attendance. Once the person begins to feel self-assured, you will find it easy to engage in conversation and you can learn a lot from the person.

Nevertheless, how you go about helping out someone with low self esteem will depend on what you want to achieve. If you are coaching a group of people so that they can excel as a team, one way of getting a shy person to engage is to direct questions at them personally in a group setup. That way, they will feel obliged to answer, and the group will benefit from the person's ideas. At the same time, you will get an opportunity to correct any ideas the person may have wrong, and the best way is, of course, to make such corrections in a subtle manner. Unless you interact carefully with the person, you could end up making them even more self-conscious than before.

8) Identify action words

Since it has been established that facial profiling is best used as part of the entire communication system, it may be a good idea to point out some verbal mannerisms of speaking that can enhance your understanding of a person.

When someone says they have done something, it is different from when the same person says they have decided to do something, and the key difference is conveyed by the word 'decided'. This is a keyword you need to take seriously in understanding the person's behavior, because it shows you the person is not rushed or impulsive but thoughtful. It also gives the notion the person is clear about what they want, and if you are trying to make a sale, your best option at this juncture may be to ask the person for their options, or what the parameters of his/her preferences are.

Thoughts on Empathy

Here in the 21st century we hear a lot of discussion on being empathic at our workplaces, school and even among friends, but what does be empathy actually mean? I want to analyze the characteristics of Empaths or empathetic people. Although, first thing we need to establish is empathy and sympathy are not the same and is often confused to be interchangeable when these two terms denote two entirely different meanings. I also want to cover the nature of Empaths, and the controversial topic if Empathy is truly genuine or a fraud?

So, what is the difference between sympathy and empathy? Sympathy is a conviction or a feeling of sorrow and compassion for the tribulations another person encounters. A perfect example of this is a world vision ad we see children in Africa, China, India and other developing countries living in poverty, and we have the feelings of pity, sorrow and even compassion elicited within us when watching these commercials for sponsorship. This is a classical example of how sympathy works. However, empathy on the other hand goes one step further than sympathy and sort of takes oneself out of our own personal lives for a moment and puts ourselves in another person's shoes who's in a plight. Empathy tends to have stronger conviction and causing people to change behavior based on emotional shifts.

An example of empathy would be your walking down the street in your neighborhood and you see a homeless man laying there on the sidewalk with a sign held up asking for food. Your first inclination is to quickly walk by him making no eye contact creating minimal interaction acting as if he isn't there. But, all of a sudden you stop yourself and think "what if that was me homeless on the street? Wouldn't I want someone to help?" At this point your conviction is so strong it moves you to change your behavior and instead of ignoring the homeless man's subtle cry for help you decide to buy him lunch. This principle of empathy is similar to the Christian religion's tenant " Do onto others as you would want done onto you", and in this sense you perceived yourself in a similar plight to the homeless man on the street, and thus you decide to help because you know if you were in the same situation you'd appreciate the help too.

Let's take a look at what Empaths actually are. Empaths are people that are intensely affected by others' emotions and have highly accurate ability to correctly perceive others and feel what they are feeling. Empaths' lives are constantly influenced by others' thoughts, desires, wishes, and moods. Being an Empath is so much more than being a highly sensitive person, and an Empath's gift isn't solely limited to simply experiencing emotional states. Empaths are similar in kind to lie detectors and are able to easily perceive other people's motivations and intentions around them.

The Nature of An Empath

Empaths take on the feelings and emotions of others around them as if the feelings were their own. This can lead to many Empaths feeling exhausted, upset, and extremely confused as they are dealing with feelings that they should not themselves be experiencing. Many Empaths experience aches and pains daily, as well as chronic fatigue issues and emotional sensitivity and it can be difficult for the Empaths to genuinely know who they are when experiencing others' feelings within themselves.

Empaths are often introverts, quiet achievers, and very expressive in emotional communication, and are very blunt, honest, and open when talking with others. They find it difficult to handle taking a compliment and prefer to give out compliments than receiving one. They can feel what is happening outside of them as opposed to what is inside of them. They are generally non-violent and non-aggressive and lean more towards embracing a peaceful lifestyle and behavior. Sometimes, the onslaught of intense feelings can make them withdraw and seek solitude for days on end. Confronting and tense situations will stress the Empaths, who seek rapid resolution of conflict wherever possible.

Empaths can build personal barriers and walls and bottle up their own emotions in an attempt to keep others from knowing their personal thoughts and feelings. The withholding of personal expression and emotions are often a resulting factor of physical and emotional abuse or neglect from a primary caregiver or a direct result of a traumatic incident. The emotional withholding is extremely detrimental to the Empaths' mental health. The Empaths need to express themselves fully, openly, and honestly to heal from any previous situations. The continuous burial of their own personal feelings only results in detrimental damage to their mental health and causes breakdowns and physical illness as well as amplification of mental illnesses.

Empaths are highly sensitive to visual stimuli such as media, books, and movies. They dislike and find it unbearable to watch forms of violence, physical or emotional pain that people inflict on others. At times, they can feel physically ill and sickened by watching such scenes. They find it difficult to comprehend or justify a person's deliberate act to intentionally cause harm to another being.

Empaths are highly inquisitive, have gentle souls, and are romantics at heart. They possess true dedication, willingness, and compassion to help people, animals, and nature. Many are highly creative, highly expressive in all creative arts, and great listeners. People around Empaths find themselves drawn like a moth to a flame – the Empaths' personalities exhibit warmth and compassion, and people are attracted to their highly magnetic traits. Complete strangers tend to fully open up to them and discuss life events and personal information that they never would normally tell anyone, let alone someone they don't know. Empaths are enthusiastic, optimistic, bubbly, and it's absolutely joyful to experience a connection with them. On the downside, since Empaths take onboard a wave of others' emotions and feelings that aren't their own, they can swing rapidly from one mood to another in an instant, leaving others around them confused or yearning to escape. Their moods can fluctuate from happy and joyful to sad and depressed in a matter of seconds.

Many Empaths are unaware of what they are experiencing – the rapid mood swings and added emotions cause a lot of confusion and distress at times. Abandoning an Empath while in the process of random mood swings can be highly detrimental. By staying with the Empath and offering love, compassion, empathy, and non-judgment can assist and guide the Empath to effectively heal and recover from previous afflictions.

Empaths are natural problem solvers and quick to come up with solutions on their feet and will often continue searching for answers until they discover a resolution. They are daydreamers, and mundane thoughts bore them. Empaths seek intelligent conversation and prefer conversations to be emotionally involving. If a teacher or tutor fails to provide adequate emotional involvement during the training, they will drift off and start daydreaming. They are most alert and aware when dealing with tutors that offer emotional and visual stimuli.

Top Traits of an Empath to Watch For

- **Knowing:** Empaths are aware of things without even being told. This ability goes well beyond intuition or gut feelings, and the more social cues the Empath seeks, the stronger this gift will become.

- **Easily Overwhelmed** Public places can sometimes be a nightmare for the Empaths to deal with. When among large crowds such as supermarkets, shopping centers, and stadiums or other large gathering locations, the vast amount of turbulent emotions from people can catch them off guard.

- **Taking Others Emotions As Their Own** The Empaths sense, feel, and take others' emotions as their own whether the person is standing by their side or hundreds of kilometers away. The more adept they become with their skills, the easier it is for them to be aware if someone is having negative thoughts about them.

- **Unable to Tolerate Violence -** The Empath cannot bear to watch any stimuli that represent violence, cruelty or tragedy. The more the Empath embraces their gift, the stronger this becomes, and many Empaths stop watching TV and reading newspapers due to this.

- **Always the Protector -** Empaths cannot stand to see anyone suffer. When they witness anyone suffering, in pain or being bullied, they will always step in to assist and protect the person in need.

- **Problem Offloading -** Not great news for the Empath – even total strangers will be drawn to them and find themselves placing their issues and worries onto them – If they're not careful and do not implement barriers, these problems can escalate and quickly become their own.

- **Naturally Drawn to Healing Roles Empaths -** are naturally drawn to holistic therapies, healing, and the metaphysical. Although many Empaths are drawn to become healers; they can often end up turning away from a healing career role despite having a natural flair and ability for it, as they often take on too much burden home from the person they are attempting to heal.

- **Creative** Empaths are highly creative and have vivid imaginations. They are drawn to roles requiring creativity such as dancing, singing, acting, drawing, and writing.

- **Love of Nature** For the Empaths, being in nature is an essential part of their lives. Having a solid love for nature and animals, Empaths and nature go hand in hand.

- **Need for Solitude** Empaths need their alone time. Often needing time to recover from the wave of emotions thrown their way by others, Empaths need quality alone time to withdraw in solitude.

Understanding Empaths and Empathy

What is the difference between being empathetic and being an Empath? Empaths are generally defined as *clairsentience*. Empaths are wired to respond to certain stimuli more responsively and with more emotion. Their gifts are energetic and psychological and can affect their bodies in a multitude of ways. Empaths are able to accurately read, understand, and experience others' emotions as if they were their own. Empathy is an ability all humans have with the exception of psychopaths. It is the ability to be able to put oneself in others' shoes to understand and view how they are feeling at that present moment, to better relate, and share what they are currently experiencing. Empathy is the ability to share in others' experiences.

It is different to being an Empath. Empaths, on the surface level, have similar feelings and attributes to having empathy. However, this is only on a surface level. Empaths have the innate and accurate ability to intuitively tune into others' emotions and feelings without needing to prompt themselves or rely on external cues to be able to do so. Having empathy is prompting yourself to understand others' feelings and emotions. The feeling of empathy requires an external trigger or event for activation, being an Empath does not.

Is Empathy Genuine or Fake?

In my final year in college I had a professor who had an interesting assertion and he challenged the class to really question if the act of empathy is something real or fake? Many of us were bewildered, but as we started to ponder and think deeper, we started to see what this professor was saying. The professor's argument was we can never truly experience what another person is going through, and thus putting ourselves in their shoes is an illusion. For instance, if you were born into an affluent family how could you empathize with someone who is homeless? It's in a sense like a fish who only knows its environmental context and experience in water and can never truly know how it is to be on dry land.

Or another way of putting it cleverly coined by *Derek Sivers* "fish don't know they're in water." A concise yet profound truth arises from this text because fish are born into water and only know the water it's surrounded by therefore, how can it comprehend anything else? How can someone who is born into a dynasty of wealth truly understand what it is to be homeless when they have never experienced it themselves? This is something I want to leave for you to ponder about for yourself. But you probably want to know my thoughts on this matter too, right?

Well, let's just say I don't completely agree with my professor who stated this assertion in my philosophy class. Although one can never truly vicariously live out someone else's unique and personal experience, we can have a certain degree of understanding of the amount of suffering they are going through. This doesn't require us to know every facet of the pain people are going through, but we can in essence metaphorically put ourselves in their shoes and look at things from the outside. Basically, getting out of ourselves, out of our self-centeredness and desires, and looking at things from a different angle. This is my personal belief on empathy, but its up to you to form your own answer. Do you lean towards what my professor was saying or maybe something along the lines of my way of thinking? – Perhaps it's a combination of both? This is up to you to figure out.

Chapter 4: Dark Psychology

Great you've made it to the 4th chapter! Now things are going to take some twists and turns as we explore the realm of the darker psychology of abnormal human nature. We've all heard of infamous serial killers from the late 1800s notorious Jack-The-Ripper, Ted Bundy, Ed Gein who was based on the story of the Texas-chain saw massacre, Tsutomu Miyazki known as the human Dracula, and I would even classify Vlad the Impaler ruler of Wallachia a psychopath due to his sadistic methods of executing prisoners or at the least possesses psychopathic tendencies.

Now I am not going to go into details of the gruesome murders and horrific acts these despicable humans have committed. But I want to discuss some of the psychological framework behind these malevolent characters. The truth is there is really no know correlation between criminal behavior and psychopathic tendencies that are linked together. Studies from various universities have undergone extensive research with some of the world's top leading psychologists studying psychopaths, and the end result or answer is something shrouded in mystery.

It has been theorized that perhaps there are different parts of the brain that are not functioning properly, thus creating these "monsters" who commit horrific acts, and yet there are some scientific studies that have determined no correlation between regions of the brain that are not functioning properly, however it is still inconclusive and there really is no definitive answer. Every psychopath has his or her own unique circumstances which contribute to their state of being. It should be noted that there have been studies showing brain scans of psychopaths and specific regions of the brain that empathy is associated too and this region normally lights up, but in psychopaths doesn't show any brain activity, thus indicating there is some sort of neurological degenerative problem of their brain functioning that is present. Ergo, most psychopaths are born not created.

Psychologists have even looked at psychopath's upbringing, and there is some merit behind this reasoning to attribute psychopathic tendencies to "nurture rather than nature". Rightfully so because some psychopaths have had very traumatized upbringings and have endured abuse and rape, but again such is not the case for all psychopaths. Unfortunately, the truth is there is no concrete evidence to definitively link psychopathic behaviours to one's upbringing or even genetics. I personally believe it's a combination of both, and my insights to this subject matter are that psychopaths are everyday people who commit horrific acts but go on life without regret or remorse. They can kill many people without a single ounce of personal conviction and go on about living their lives as if nothing happened.

Its more of a darker state of being also influenced by there abnormal desires whether necrophilia, sadism, and even cannibalism. The epitome of both genetic and environmental moral degradation, perhaps a mistake brought by nature, yet there is no true way of certainly knowing what causes psychotic behaviors.

The good news is there are ways of analyzing and identifying who is a psychopath or sociopath in modern society. Popular to contrary beliefs psychopaths don't come off as "scary" in the public eye, and they certainly would not want to give themselves away by appearing in a repulsive demeanor. Psychopaths have an uncanny ability to attract people through charm, manipulate them, posses hallmark signs of the lack thereof empathy or remorse, absent moral compass, and can even be very attractive! These are the classical traits of a psychopathic tendencies that we have acquired over years of study and a body of scientific evidence.

Whether they behave out of boredom, lack of purpose, excitement for causing pain, mutilation or manipulating others, the bottom line is psychopaths have very high social intelligence and know how to create appeal through body language and their mannerisms. There are psychopaths who are more reclusive or introverted in nature who are a lot easier to spot and rather than create trust and than murder, they kidnap their victims and unleash their evil on them. I can go on and on about the reasons behind what makes them tick, perhaps they just desire to be acknowledged by society hence why some of them even communicate or taunt law enforcement through leaving behind letters and cryptic clues.

Difference Between Psychopaths, Narcists and Sociopaths

There is definitely an overlap of character traits between these terms, however many people use these names interchangeably when they do not hold the same exact meanings. So, the first thing you should know is that every psychopath is narcistic, but not every narcissist is a psychopath! Let's define a narcists; a narcist can be defined as one who has an excessive interest in oneself and physical appearance. We see many narcissists today at the workplace, on television, in Hollywood, and even within your social circles. A narcissist only has his or her own best interest at heart and only lives for selfish ambitions. But remember this doesn't mean they posses' psychopathic tendencies, so don't go calling the cops on them because you find them pompous. Narcissistic traits can be exhibited by self-entitlement, lack of empathy, ostentatiousness and need for self-validation.

Therefore, when a narcist does something wrong he or she does feel a certain degree of remorse and shame, but they feel more shame than guilt because shame is a publicly induced emotion and they're more concerned with public perception than personal guilt. A Psychopath on the other hand is an entirely different beast and they're essentially the combination of both traits of narcissists and sociopaths with the added elements of lacking empathy or remorse, and perhaps have some sort of abnormal desire to elicit pain, sadism, and cannibalism.

Now let's look at sociopaths. Sociopaths are similar to psychopaths, but are not born, they are created by their environment. Therefore, environmental conditioning is what creates these types of people, imagine children who grow up in a rough neighborhood, and thus have criminal elements in their behavior, commits violence, steals, arson, and vandalizes public property. Imagine if you live a certain lifestyle of lawlessness for a long enough time you eventually adapt to it and therefore take up these negative characteristics.

Anti-Social Behavior

Not all anti social behavior exhibited by someone makes them a psychopath. There are numerous definitions of what anti-social behaviors entail, and I will go into detail of the most accurate meaning of this term. I see this term often thrown around carelessly and even to the point where some people misunderstand the whole concept and as a result mislabel other individuals, especially children.

A child who is rambunctious and doesn't want to conform to school rules in regard to staying quite in class while the teacher is talking, running around, but does not cause harm to others is not an anti-social child nor posses these tendencies. Sadly, I see teachers misdiagnosing children who fall into this category which is a real disservice and injustice towards children and society. Perhaps you've even seen it yourself people labeling children whom isolate themselves as "anti-social" when in fact they're simply introverted and have social anxiety.

There's a distinction in psychology between anti-social and asocial behavior, anti-social behavior requires a person to cause harm to others verbally or physically without having regret or remorse, and asocial behavior entails isolating oneself from others and must not be mistaken for anti-social tendencies. There is a danger with a misdiagnosis of children and unfortunately these misdiagnoses are a reality and exist today in the modern world. Someone who doesn't like to talk to others is asocial and many times gets mislabelled being anti-social because of the misinformation mainstream media promotes.

Anti-social personality disorder is when a person lacks a moral compass or conscious of his or her wrong doing to others. This abnormal mentality which creates destructive patterns of behavior to others could be violence, vandalism, bullying, stealing, and other destructive tendencies. The manifestation of this personality disorder usually occurs during early childhood to late adolescence. People who posses anti-social behavior often resists authority, exploit and manipulate others for their own personal self-interest. Just like psychopaths the exact cause of anti-social personality disorder (ASPD) is unknown as there are many factors involved such as genetics, upbringing, and context. Males have a stronger inclination towards this particular personality disorder because of the hormone testosterone which naturally makes males more aggressive. The likelihood of ASPD increases in individuals who have had exposure to abusive upbringings, parents who have had ASPD, and alcoholism. Behavior from children who display ASPD can range from cruelty to animals, arson, vandalism and even violence. The common denominator here that makes anti-social people and psychopaths the way they are is there lack of remorse of their actions. However, people struggling with ASPD do have the capacity to exhibit genuine empathy to a certain degree.

From a psychological standpoint being anti-social and a psychopath is not the same, however they posses very similar traits. From my personal observations and experience I would say having ASPD is the gateway to becoming a full fledge psychopath. Therefore, it is important to seek treatment if you know anyone who struggles with ASPD because without intervention there is potential for ASPD to evolve into full blown psychopathy.

The line can be almost blurred at times when trying to identify a person who is anti-social versus psychopathy, but as always when analyzing people, you must consider the context of the situation whether its current circumstances or past history these all need to be held into account for you to make an appropriate appraisal of an individual's mental state. The biggest markers or hallmarks of a psychopath is extreme malevolence towards others, and lack of empathy and remorse for their actions. While ASPD individuals have a certain degree of malevolence, lack of remorse but can exhibit empathy at times. But the burning question for you to ponder about is what differentiates someone who is experiencing ASPD due to personal life problems versus early signs of psychopathy?

Now on the other side of the spectrum asocial behavior is characterized by the deliberate avoidance of social interaction. People who are asocial can be inconsiderate and hostile toward other people. Individuals who fall under this psychological disorder usually have personality disorders, depression, schizophrenia, social anxiety and even autism.

Are You Dating a Narcissist?

How do you identify if your dating a narcissist? This is more common than you think, and I've come across married couples who come into therapy because both husband and wife struggle with narcissism! In this section I want to provide you the insights on analyzing narcissists and quickly identifying them, so you can save face, avoid heart break and other grievances. Right off that bat I want to say if your dating a narcissist do yourself a favor and end the relationship and any connection you may have to them because you're only asking for trouble the longer you entertain this type of toxic relationship. Remember to a lesser degree being a narcissist is a type of personality disorder and being in a relationship with someone with a mentally abnormal state of mind beckons trouble.

You probably think well if I was dating a narcissist I would know, right? But you see things aren't always that simple because there are many concealing devices that narcissist have that can create attraction and appeal, thus making you overlook their negative personality. Believe it or not there are a lot of celebrities who are narcissists! This goes for actors, models, athlete, musicians, artists and other performers as well. There is a huge possibility that at one point or another in your life perhaps you've looked up to a narcissist too.

But what are these devices they use to conceal their negative personality of narcissism? The answer is quite simple and is right under our noses! Vanity is apart of what makes up a narcissist and this usually stems from physical attractiveness, wealth, high social status, and even intelligence. These are all superficial devices that narcissist use to hide their narcissism. How do they do it? Well, its not a question of how they do it, but why we as humans are so captivated by physical beauty, wealth, and social status?

Think about it the narcissists are caught up in their own vanity and sub-consciously know that using these types of devices attract people to them. We see singers, politicians, Instagram models and even some of our friends exhibiting narcissism that use their superficial devices as a platform to gratify acknowledgement and self-worth from society.

Narcissists are not born but are created by the conditioning of their situational context. They do poorly in relationships because they are to busy self-gratifying and have tunnel vision mentality. They are not really wired for empathy, compassion or sympathy. Most narcissist won't admit to being self-loathing and lovers of themselves, and this is due to negativity that the label connotes. Depending on the level of narcissism one exhibits they may not be fit for child rearing or parenting duties because they would neglect their children and focus on themselves. They don't grasp the law of reciprocity, for instance if you were to have a conversation with a narcissist you would find it one sided. The hallmark signs you are talking to a narcissist is when the conversation revolves only around themselves, they are the center of attention, and they never consider asking your opinion or consider how your doing. They're intent is just to use you as a social validation vehicle for self-acknowledgement.

But the question is now how do we tell the difference between narcissist and self-confident people. There is definitely a line to be crossed but the question is wherein lies that line? There is a rule of thumb I go by and that is narcissistic people tend to be arrogant as well, and thus claim to know it all and have seen it all. If you cannot find an ounce of reverence to how infinitesimal we are to the universe or if they cannot concede to how vast the universe is in the grand scheme of things, then there is a high chance the person you are dealing with is a narcissist.

Now don't get confused with healthy validation where people want to be acknowledged which is completely normal. But narcissism in it of itself is the lack of empathy towards others and holds the self as the epi-center of the universe. If a person genuinely works hard and creates value for people through their dedication, and is only acknowledged because of the value they created, then that person is not a narcissist as long as they don't require the self-validation of others for normal every day things. For example, if your writing a book that is truly of value to people and you receive praise and critical acclaim you in return get well deserved validation, but this doesn't make you a narcissist. It's when you start writing mediocre books that don't serve your audience's needs and is self-centered towards yourself, and only you perceive it as good work that's the M.O. of a narcissistic person.

Therefore, in essence a narcissistic person's self-esteem is an illusion in it of itself because it requires the validation of others to exist as oppose to having self-esteem based on your own personal development.

Narcissism and Technology

Does the advent of technologies such as social media and other communication platforms amplify narcissism? Absolutely yes! Narcissism has been 10x and magnified manifold ever since we've been given the access to the internet. We can see it all the time in everyday examples such as Snapchat, Facebook, Instagram, Twitter, and even YouTube.

Facebook, Snapchat & Instagram – Arguably the greatest top 3 social media platforms of our time. Most people are found utilizing these 3 platforms in our society, especially here in the western hemisphere. These platforms thrive on vanity and self-indulgence, and one cannot deny that attention is the new currency or some call it the new drug. When others like your photos or posts you get a surge of euphoria because it's a feel good experience that another person is validating you. This happens equally between men and women and we see this manifest in different forms, for men they post pictures either of their new car, vacation, and physique. Women on the other hand tend to post more scantly provocative pictures of themselves that garner the attention of others to validate them, and as well as vacation life experiences.

There's nothing inherently wrong posting about your car, body image, and vacation experience. However, in the end it sums down to your motive and if your intent is to achieve some type of social validation or self-worth approval from others to uphold your self-esteem than you may very well be a narcissist. But if its to truly share your life's experiences with others and capturing the highlight moments of your life through social media than its completely healthy.

How to Deal With Judgemental People

Have you ever come across people who are just way to judgemental? I think we all know that grouchy person who is quick to judge, and yet sometimes their judgements can also be hypocritical as well too. Whether high school, college or at the workplace judgemental people exist in every facet of our lives, but how do we deal with these types of people? There is a few mental strategies you can use to help mitigate their negativity so it doesn't effect your personal well being.

The first thing you need to realize is not to take their criticism personally, and this may seem like a daunting task since were not machines who can just block out their statements at a given command. This does require a certain degree of mental fortitude, but even better you should realize that judgemental people are not only judging you they also judge other groups of people too given the chance, thus you are not alone or being singled out.

Secondly what you need to do is take a step outside of yourself and employ empathy. Do this so you can get to the reason of why this person is judgemental to you? Could it be their personal upbringing, maybe their perfectionists, or perhaps even hold insecurities and project judgements onto you to compensate for their inadequacies.

Thirdly you need to associate with more people who bring the best out of you, motivate you, encourage and support you. Limit the time you spend with judgemental people if you can as you don't need that emotional toxicity in your life. Surround yourself with positive minded people who won't bring you down. Spend your time and energy with people who have your best interest at heart and not ulterior motives.

Fourthly set boundaries! You need to stand-up for yourself if your being emotionally abused. You need to set the limit before you hit the breaking point and have a mental break down. There is nothing wrong with putting your foot down so long as you don't create a conflict. Perhaps, you can say something like "I don't appreciate your unconstructive comments that only serve to tear me down, please don't talk to me if you have nothing good to say." A statement like that should be able to give the critic a reality cheque and make them back off from any future verbal assaults. Remember be diplomatic as being hostile towards your critic may further exasperate the problem and by showing diplomacy you show to others you're the bigger person.

Do You Really Know Who Your Real Friends Are?

This is not a trick question. But do you really know who your real friends are and how to spot "fake friends". I want to really challenge you to think deeply and become self-aware of who you associate with and why? Do you enjoy their companionship? Or do you associate with your friends because you have a vested interest? And vice-versa why does your friend hang around you? There is always an underlying value proposition or value system which dictates the motives of your friendship. Some friends can be more genuine than others, and some are closer while others are more of the seasonal type friends.

Obviously not all friends are made equal. But did you know you could have toxic friends within your social circle and not even know? Perhaps they just hang around you to fill the void of loneliness, but is quick to judge, never encourages the best for you, holds grudges, and perhaps even jealous of you. Having a friend who is blunt and gives you constructive criticism is different than a friend who just "hates" on you. Usually friends who only have negative things to say about your lifestyle have their own personal insecurities to deal with and thus try to elevate themselves by putting you down. Some may even boast and lie about the things they are capable of and have a skewed perception of themselves in relation to you.

The best way to spot fake friends is if they do the following; 1. Do not encourage your achievements or success, 2. Motivate you to be better, 3. If they always have to try to one up you and show you that their life is better, 4. Anti-social tendencies to disagree with everything you say just for the sake of disagreement, 5. Rub your shortcoming in your face by telling you they would never make the same mistakes, and 6. Passive aggressive in conversation.

I want to share a story with you. I had a friend named Joel years ago back in my first year of college I knew him for quite a number of years you could say we were childhood friends, and pretty close friends in elementary school. I notice anytime we hung out he had a strange predilection to disagree with everything I said for the sake of debating and to prove he was knowledgeable, when in most cases he was absolutely in the wrong. Why I didn't stop associating myself with him is something I wish I could answer. Not only was he anti-social, but anytime I had a positive story to share he always responded by fabricating his own stories to one up me, and on top of that didn't really encourage my success, but I noticed anytime I mentioned something good that happened to me in my life such as new job that paid better I observed micro-facial expressions that one could notably tell jealously was brewing in his heart. Reluctant to say words of encouragement or positivity, anti-social tendencies, and jealously are all hallmark signs of a fake friend.

After a while I got irritated and asked the advice of another close friend, John who was also a psychology major but in his 2nd year, and I told him my dilemma. I expressed my deep dislike for Joel as he seemed very passive aggressive towards me. John pointed something out I should have realized, Joel was an awkward friend (note John knew Joel from childhood too), he grew up being the "fall guy" for ridicule and was made the laughing stock of our school growing up. But I was one of the only friends that showed him kindness and a measure of empathy, and John also noted the fact that nobody else really kept in touch with Joel after graduation, and also the fact that he was severely overweight, and this does have detrimental effects to people psychologically.

Therefore, I realized all of his negative traits really stemmed from his own personal insecurities which he projected onto me through anti-social behavior. This is a classical real life example of what some of the fake friends within your own social circle may look like. Now the value system here between us was he hung out with me because I was kind, compassionate and empathetic, and I associated myself with him because of sentimental reasons as I knew him for a very long time. By this point I realized a very valuable lesson and that is that it really doesn't matter how long you've known your friends for that doesn't define a real friend. But what does define a real friend is the value system they hold and what they can add or contribute to your life. I'm not being cynical here, but life is a give and take policy if your friends are taking more than they are giving, than I would strongly suggest you find a new group of people to associate with.

Why would you be friends with someone who only calls when he or she needs a favor? Perhaps its not a favor, but they just need to vent to you about their life's struggle and in a sense use you for "free emotional therapy". My message is just be careful with who you call your friends, who you associate with and who you spend your time with. You must identify the motives of your friends right from the get-go in order to spot *phoniness*.

Chapter 5 Personality Types

How would you identify your personality type? Would you say your rather rash, reckless, impulsive or perhaps clam, cool and collective? The concept of personality types is something we've been trying to decipher since ancient times, and there are many theories behind it. There are different techniques and tools we can use to measure one's personality, and although not black and white it really boils down to the burning question is what makes up the "self ". The self can be thought as the cohesive entity that consist of personality, actions, feelings and beliefs which all contribute to our personality, and which make us who we are. But to be honest this becomes quite convoluted because the self cannot really be quantified or measured, and there are other factors such as genetics, environment and social conditioning that also come into play as well. There really is no concrete unanimously agreed upon answer from all fronts that can really determine what the self is. It is still an enigma shrouded in mystery.

We keep trying to box people into categories as soon as we meet them. We try to find the right tags for people we come across. A jabbering guy would be termed extrovert while a shy guy would be given the tag of an introvert. Human behavior has always been the subject of great wonder and study. It has got layers to it. The surface is barely scratched when we categorize people as introvert or extrovert.

Certain tests may help you determine various aspects of one's personality. Personalities are not binary; they have several facets to them. It is utterly naive to expect human personalities to be one-dimensional. It is only by asking questions that we can arrive at an answer that has been attempted from various angles, thereby allowing us a holistic view of something as grand as human personality.

Trait Theory

Instead of associating personality types to lingering sub-conscious drives, influences or genetic disposition *trait theory* breaks down personality types by defining personality through stable and lasting behaviors we make volitionally. Our personality can determine our day to day average behavior but is not a definitive indicator of determining what we will do in an unpredictable circumstance. Psychologist *A. Bandura* came up with a different theory known as the *social cognitive perspective*, and this theory emphasized that humans learn behavior by observing and imitating their social surroundings, thus in other words shape shifting their personality and even appearances to suit their environments like a chameleon.

There is a saying that the sum 3 total of your closet friends defines who you are and in the theory of social cognitive perspective it states that because you volitionally choose to be in a certain environmental context and the environmental context itself shapes, moulds and influences your personality these are two reciprocal exchanges of determining factors that make up your personality. They work together kind of like the ying and the yang to make up who you are or what defines you.

Point of Control

Poetically put humans are the navigators of their souls and creator of their roads, by which means we are both the creators and products of the environmental context we surround ourselves with. Therefore, our sense of personal control also plays a factor in determining our personality types. For instance, someone who is bold and believes they can carve their owns destiny and navigate their faith through their actions and beliefs is someone who has an "internal point of control", and on the opposite side of the spectrum someone who believes that their life is solely guided by an external force and their destiny is predetermined meaning they have little to no control, this means that this person has an "external point of control".

Extroverts vs. Introverts

Introverts are people who take their sweet time responding to a particular question. They wait to receive the full information about the question so asked. They are not impatient to jump to answering as soon as a substantial portion of the question is over. They calmly wait until the question is over, ask whether there is a follow-up to it or not and then spend another two minutes to frame their response. This is the ideal way to describe how an introvert's response goes.

On the other hand, an extrovert would launch into answering-mode even before you have finished your question. They would appear excited to tell you every single thing they know about the subject of the question. They may not even wait for you to catch a gasp. They will simply talk over you and shut you up in case you seem to protest their sudden intrusion into the proceedings. It is in their nature to impose their knowledge upon unsuspecting victims.

You must have come across people who label you as either an introvert or an extrovert. Stay away from such labeling practices. It is very easy to make a first impression of a person and tag them under either of these categories. However, learn the art of delving further into the human mind. There are very few people who are completely either of the two. We tend to imbibe into ourselves a little bit of both the boxes. We often adjust ourselves according to the situation, and that is the best way to go about it.

Take your time to reach a conclusion regarding someone's introvert or extrovert nature. Not all people wear their emotions on their sleeves. They keep them hidden inside their innermost mental treasuries. It may take a while to read people's intentions before you make a call.

Sensing vs. Intuition

Another way to assess human personalities is to check what they are most fascinated by - the past, the present or the future. It's not just about being fascinated with one of the three; it also includes being obsessed with and living one's life by them.

People who like to live in the moment and focus on what's going on right now are called Sensors. They tend to not worry too much about what is going to happen. They are rather concentrated on what is real and happening right under their noses.

Sensors are not just focused on the present. They also take into account the past. They believe in the idea of learning from your mistakes and using the lessons so learned to gain something valuable for the future. Though future does feature in the grand scheme of things, in the end, it is not an important spoke in the wheel. Sensors use their previous experience to march ahead. Despite everything being about the future eventually, the future does not play as relevant a part as the past and the present does.

On the other hand, we have the Intuitive people. These people are usually focused on what is going to happen in the coming days, years or decades. They plan ahead and do not let the past affect anything in the foreseeable future. They seem to be less practical than the other herd, but their ideology does make sense at a certain level. Ask a Sensor to describe their favorite politician, and they will dig up the history of the concerned politician, their current policies and the current role they are playing in the world politics. However, ask the same question to an Intuitive person, and he is most likely to answer all the long-term benefits of electing the said politician and how he could prove to be a good leader in the future. The primary difference between the two groups could be best described by the above illustration.

Thinking vs. Feeling

The feelers will always take into consideration the impact their actions and words have on those watching them. They are pretty mindful of who is watching and what sort of an impression the crowd is going to take back home. They can be expected to be careful while speaking. You will see them picking the correct words to say something. Political correctness is present in high amounts in their speech and action.

On the contrary, thinkers do not believe in the concept of being considerate towards others. They will call a spade a spade. They are of the firm view that public morality should not be hindered by thoughts. Tact is something the thinkers find hard to imbibe in their personalities.

The Architect

The Architects are often hailed as bookworms pretty early in their lives. They have ambitions but often choose to pursue them in private. They are dreamers yet know how to add a dash of practicality to the same. They are curious about everything they come across and leave no stone unturned to gain knowledge whenever it is made available.

The Logician

Fiercely competitive and amazingly creative, the Logicians are known to be good human lie detectors. They can make a guess when the person talking to them is not sure of what he's saying. The Logicians usually use their friends as guniea pigs to test their half-formed theories. They are constantly trying to spot patterns in places that offer none.

The Commander

Among all, this is the person who will take a stand, put his foot down and lead the pack back home. He/She is the lone beacon of hope in a stormy night. This individual is strong-willed, intelligent and willing to take bold decisions when the situation so requires. They love a good challenge and do not back off when adversities pile on. They can often come across as too loud and dominating, and perhaps even obnoxious. However, when allowed to become the leader of the group, they can take charge from the front.

The Debater

The Debaters are the most analytical sorts. They would not take an issue lying down. The pros and cons of a subject are well assessed and processed through their mental faculties before they formulate an argument. If you tell them a fact, they won't accept it right away. They will do a fair amount of research and attempt to disapprove an already established and recognized postulate.

The Advocate

The Advocates are the most argumentative type of the lot. Much like the debaters, they won't accept a fact for what it is. They have solid opinions about issues they connect with on an emotional level. They are the ones who are ready to take bold decisions and stick to it throughout. They may not be as vocal about their views in public as they may be in private.

The Mediator

Out of all the personality types, this is the most helpful one. They are always engrossed in their daydreams while at the same time being aware of what's going on around them. They may not come across as observational due to their delusional selves, but they are always watching. They have a tendency to reduce their keen observations into writing, which also explains why a lot of this personality type end up becoming poets and authors.

The Protagonist

The talker of the group, the Protagonist, leads from the front and hogs the limelight of a room right away. He or she does not shy away from expressing oneself. The best way to describe this personality type is the phrase "speak before you think." Often times he may end up making a fool out of himself, but that does not prevent them from being blunt about their opinions.

The Campaigner

These are the socially aware people among the group. They will keep their peers updated about what's happening in the society while vehemently taking a cause seriously. They are always eager to help those who are in dire need. They care about their causes a lot and hence can be seen marching in parades and protests.

The Logistician

This group of individuals is all about facts. They rely more on statistics than emotions. They won't mind throwing an algorithm book on your face if you try to gain a higher ground in an argument by citing humanitarian reasons. They keep a group grounded by sticking to scientific empirical evidence and numbers.

The Defender

They are the folks who stay very much connected to their loved ones. They do not care whether the people they love are wrong. If they are in trouble, the Defenders will risk everything to bail them out. It does not matter to a Defender whether the people they care about have been defaulters. The emotion of care is strong with this group.

The Executive

Some people are just good at managing things and people. These are the Executives. They may not be the most intelligent bunch of the lot, but when it comes to organizational skills, no one can beat them. They know how to handle things and create a smooth pathway for them to run. Being a natural at management skills, it is their pleasure when they are asked to look after stuff like gatherings, events, and meetings. Their strengths lie in coordinating dynamics, logistics management and allocating resources.

The Consul

If there is one trait that sets apart the people from this group, it is Popularity. These folks comprise of the cheerleading teams and the basketball players. They have a social influence that is unparalleled. They may not initiate or continue an intellectual conversation, but they are amazing at encouraging people to do the same. You won't find such people being sarcastic, witty or quick to provide a retort. They are simple folks who just want to grab the limelight.

The Virtuoso

People belonging to this group can often be seen playing with things. The engineers, musicians, mechanics and builders all belong to this type. These groups of people are usually talented in the fine arts, music, playing instruments, etc. If they do not like the make and build of a structure, they will want to make it better by dismantling it and putting it back together, except in a better way this time around. They take the risk of being different by defying the set standards of beauty and arrangement. They experiment with what has always been there.

The Adventurer

You cannot put these folks in a box. You can never find them working a cubicle job. They feel suffocated sitting at a desk, trying to draft an agreement that they don't even have an interest in. They want to explore the world and see places. They want to experiment with the society and defy all the conventions. There is an element of spontaneity in them, and that is what makes them quick on their feet. They are the first ones to raise hands for a trekking trip with friends.

The Entrepreneur

You can spot them at parties, self-made mindset, walking from one group of friends to another. They can never stay in one place to listen to the latest political news. They would rather talk about things that are artsy, flamboyant and superfluous. They have traits of a leader and desire independence, and believe in working for themselves and providing services as oppose to work for an employer.

The Entertainer

The life of the party, in its true sense, is the Entertainer. They are full of energy as they talk, sing, dance, and gossip their way around the group. They do not give a damn about who is listening to them. Their sole purpose of the day is to please and interact with as many people as it is possible for them.

Which category do you fall under? It is very much possible that you may find yourself listed under more than one. Human personalities are a funny business; it will take you more than one guess to reach a conclusion. I hope you were able to relate to at least one of the aforementioned categories.

Judging vs. Perceiving

Take the following illustration into consideration:

Jack and Jill are sitting in their bedroom, getting hungry with every passing minute. Jack gets up, and says, "Hey, how about we get ourselves some food?" Jill agrees that the hunger needs to be attended to. Jack suggests that they go to a Chinese restaurant, to which Jill agrees again. Jack changes into a pair of jeans, and turns around, beaming, "You know what! That Italian restaurant has some nice desserts, and it's a weekend discount they're offering these days. How about we go there instead?" Jill, taken aback, replies," I thought we were going to the Chinese place for dinner."

Are you Jack from the above illustration? If your answer is yes, then you are a perceiver. You take life as it comes to you. You roll with the wind and do not obsess over set plans much. You believe in not letting decided routes ruin your journey. You are willing to, as Robert First would call it, take the route less traveled.

Are you Jill from the illustration? You are a hard to please person. You do not like making changes to a plan that has been mutually agreed to all members of your group. You want to go through a well thought-out plot only because it was the first one that also happened to get to a majority vote of approval.

The diplomats

The personality of the diplomat will be a little less pushy than that of the analyzer. These are people who are likely to do more listening, but you will notice that they are reserved and tend not to speak when they don't need to. Happy and practical, these folks are the ones who know who they are. They tend to sit quietly in the limelight, but are not afraid to come up with solutions when these are needed and are likely to be the kind of people who are able to compromise to please others. They might also have their own agendas and will cheerfully lead you toward their aims without being pushy about it.

The sentinels

When you meet characters like this, you are in no doubt at all about who is in control. The sentinels are smart, sharp and know what they are talking about. They yield authority. These are people who can delegate without a pause because they are in the know and will always choose those most capable of doing what is being requested of them. If you meet one of these, you will definitely get the impression that you are in the presence of someone in authority and their body language will be such that no one will doubt that authority. They also have a tendency to make people around them feel comfortable and will not misuse their authority. Thus, they emit the feeling that they can be trusted and mean what they say.

The Exploratory Character

You can usually tell this kind of character from a distance. These are people who may not conform to the usual approach. Their characteristics will be bold and noticeable but not in the same way as the sentinels. They are happy to experiment and to try new things. Examples of characters that would fit into this personality profile would be entrepreneurs who are willing to take chances. They are flamboyant and you will notice they are likely to be surrounded by people who are enthused by them.

The first impression that you have of anyone depends upon your background as well as theirs. You have certain expectations of people and not everyone is going to fit the mold. The wider you travel, the easier it is to distinguish the different characters that pass through your life, since you will have been exposed to many kinds and may not have taken much notice in the past.

However, if you truly want to be able to read people and analyze what they stand for, it may be worthwhile observing people in a neutral area and trying to categorize them so that you get more experienced at recognizing each of the types. This helps you to be able to deal with people in the future, based upon what you learn simply from looking at them for the first time.

Conclusion

You are a combination of all of the above-mentioned human traits and personalities. You, as a human, cannot be summed up in either black or white; you are *"grey"*. It is only when all the above categorizations are taken into account that a fair understanding of what personality type you are comes to the fore.

Chapter 6: How To Influence Anyone?

There are several ways to influence people which both consist of verbal and non verbal means. I want to discuss some of the non verbal methodologies master practitioners employ on people. The human brain dislikes discord and gravitates towards serenity and harmony. Calm, cool and collective is what our body language should emanate because people are drawn towards this.

Mirroring

When engaging anyone you want to mirror their state of being. If they're stressed, angry, or sad you want to be able to create a personal connection to them by also drawing from your past experiences and subtly expressing the same emotions they are going through. Remember people ultimately want to communicate and be understood, and even if they might be on the wrong side of the conflict you don't necessarily have to agree with them, but you can understand them from their point of view. Don't omit the truth but grasp there thought process and appreciate their perspective.

Humans are impressionable beings and are easily influenced by others, especially those who appear to be in positions of authority hold strong influence, such as celebrities, singers, performers, and athletes. Influence occurs within every facet of society from macro level to our small social circles, when people see you picking up garbage around your neighborhood, they'll start doing the same, and when you start dumping garbage without a care leaving a mess they'll follow in tandem. If you speak a certain way or use a stylish tone people will start picking up on that and reciprocating that behavior. You start using foul language and the people around you will eventually start doing the same! – Why does happen?

This social phenomenon arises because people don't want to feel left out or ostracized deep down inside sub-consciously, so instead they follow as a result due to the fact that they want to belong. Humans are social creatures and thrive off companionship and the last thing anyone wants is to feel like is the "other". This is quite similar to the "*Jones Effect*", which is a philosophy that states that people sub-consciously have this perception that they must keep up or compete with their neighbors in regards to material goods and socio-economic status, and by falling short of the social class benchmark you are perceived as inferior both socio-economically.

We can see this at play all the time here in North America. Your neighbor gets some renovations done, roofing, kitchen upgrades, or perhaps a new pool in the backyard. The first instinct you have is to mirror or one up your neighbor by acquiring something similar in perceived value or greater. By engaging in this behavior, you are trying to proof your self-worth from a social class and socio-economic perspective.

The thing is people do this without even realizing it because this occurs sub-consciously. This can happen anywhere, and this doesn't necessarily only pertain to your neighbor for this social phenomenon to arise. In fact, this happens at work among your co-workers as well, from clothing, new cars and vacations. How many times have you been influenced because your co-worker went on vacation and had an amazing experience, and now you want to do the same or even better, so you can flaunt and share your experiences too.

Curiosity Builds Rapport

Earlier in the book I discussed how using elements of curiosity can help you have a more extensive analysis of a person. But curiosity can also be employed when you are trying to influence people.

To first influence someone there are a few points in the criteria that you must meet before they shift over to your side. People must feel 1. Validated, 2. Persuaded, and 3. Have a genuine connection.

Validated - People want to feel important because its in human nature to desire be the center of the world. By neglecting the importance people have and their contribution to society regardless of how small it is you in effect negate their sense of self-worth and belonging. I am not saying you need to inflate people's egos with false notions or perceptions of themselves, however given the chance you need to acknowledge their stance and appreciate their position in society. – From the smallest cogs to the biggest gears.

Persuaded – You can find several books on the art of persuasion. There are various methods to get someone to do what you want, and in this case your trying to persuade someone to divulge more personal information about themselves so you can analyze them better. Persuasion often times is thought to be like manipulation and there are some overlapping characteristics that both these techniques have, however at the end of the day your motive is what will determine if your trying to persuade for good reason or manipulate people out of malice. I want to give you an in-depth overview of persuasion and the many aspects to it.

Social Proof - Social proof is a tactic used a lot in the marketing space and this simply means having some sort of validation or proof of concept that a proposition works. For instance, on infomercials weight loss gurus try to sell you their programs and they use themselves and other testimonials as social proof to reinforce that fact that their program (which is the proposition) actually works and there are real people who have achieved real results. By showing you the results either on themselves and other customers they prove to you that they have the results you want. This tool works very well in persuading people to do things, such as buying a weight loss program.

Establish Authority - The fact is people tend to be persuaded easier by people in positions of authority. This phenomenon occurs primarily because of the power dynamics between the "influencer" and the "influenced". People in positions of authority are put on a pedestal by society and they appear to be "super human" at times due to the authority and strong presence they have created. Society wants to belong and tends to be attracted to people who posses' success, and symbols of success which can be attributed to wealth, exotic cars, attractive women or men, and other accomplishments that society values.

The irony here is its us the people of society who give people in authority their power! We feed the notion that a certain individual is above and beyond 99% of the population when the truth is were all mortal human beings at the end of the day, and share the same afflictions, pains, joys, suffering, and other human tendencies too. In a sense its sort of an illusion that society creates and becomes bound too. By establishing authority, you make the persuasion process easier because you built trust with someone who relies on your reputation as the reason, he or she should concede to you.

Speak In a Concise & Simple Manner - Using text book knowledge or advanced vocabulary when talking to the average person for the purpose of persuasion is one of the biggest mistakes you can make! This does not create an appeal nor an advantage for you, but on the contrary is a repellent and turns people off because you appear to be pompous, conceited and in over your head. Not only that but this can be quite intimidating and condescending to others, thus the importance of keeping things to the point and use language easily understood by the majority of the populace. Remember when your trying to persuade someone you want them to grasp the conversation at hand, and there is no benefit using complex jargon.

I had a friend back in high school who was a bright kid and he excelled academically in all subject matters. However, when it came to finding a job during summer break, he appeared to have a real hard time doing so. The reason why was because when he got his interviews, he would condescend the interviewer by academic jargon and boast about his accomplishments. This obviously did not resonate with the interviewer and as a result he failed to persuade the interviewer to give him a job opportunity. A great lesson can be learned from this real life scenario because what this shows is why concise and simple language is better than taking the convoluted approach when trying to persuade someone. Clearly the interviewer was not fond of his advances using jargon, and on top of that bragging about his accomplishments.

Humility is key and is something we can all use in our daily lives, remember pride comes before the fall as the saying goes, and in this case study we can see a prideful student although qualified taking a big fall and as a result lost many job opportunities. Ultimately, keep things in its context please as I don't want you going for an interview for a job that requires some advanced or technical knowledge and going in with the mindset to use simple and concise language. The situations vary, and common sense would dictate that if your going in for a job that requires higher qualifications you want to use terminology that suits that position. – Remember that friend I mentioned was applying to basic entry level positions.

Utilize Extreme Words – There really is no formal text book definition of this term, however I'm going to define it for you for the purpose of this book. When I say use extremes words, I am referring to words like best, largest, greatest, worst, smallest and least. Its proven that using these types of words when trying to convince someone is effective because when you add these words in conversation you have the person thinking of that extreme word you utilized in regard to its context or situation. For example, you go into a car dealership and your looking for a new car, and the sales man approaches you and he tells you all the features of the car and mentions the car uses the best state of the art technology and artificial intelligence capabilities on the market for self-driving, self parking, and other automated technological features.

You are now more likely going to buy that car because this salesman whether his statements were true or not used an extreme word which painted a vivid picture for you in your mind, and in this case, it was the "best". Ergo, you end up signing a finance deal and successfully purchase a new car, but what you don't realize is this salesman has subtly persuaded you using one of the extreme word's technique.

Another example on the opposite extreme could be you go into the health and food store and ask the clerk what you can do to reverse your arthritis. So, the clerk asks you a simple question which is "what's your diet like?" and you tell her bread, pasta, pastries and a whole bunch of other refined carbs. Thus, she responds by telling you that this is the **worst** thing you can do for your health. Than she gives you the remedy and bunch of supplements you should take. The key extreme word used here in this scenario was worst which connotes extreme negativity and has captured your attention by triggering your consciousness to realize that your behavior is not good and implies it needs to be changed.

Urgency- This is a classic tactic used by marketers. This method creates an impression that something won't last or your going to run out of time if you don't act now. This sense of urgency is used during boxing day, Christmas and other holiday seasons to captivated customers to purchase products fast because the deal won't be there forever. This simple marketing tactic has generated over millions of dollars in revenue for so many companies worldwide because it exploits our human psychology by making us feel like we are going to miss out on a big opportunity if we do not act fast. So, the next time you see a "limited time offer" you know what faculty of persuasion is being used!

Have a Genuine Connection- Lastly, in order to influence someone, you need to have a genuine personal connection. The biggest brands in history have all created some level of connection to their customers' personally, culturally, etc and therefore they still stand till this day. Companies know that in order to have repeat buyers willing give them money they must create trust, and in order to achieve trust they must first establish a genuine connection.

How do you establish a connection? People will be attracted to you when you can appeal to them by having some sort of relatability, reference point, answer to their problem, or some sort of cultural context. By using one the elements discussed to create a genuine connection and have a stronger chance of influencing them. For example, Sprite one of the biggest soft drink brands that exists uses a personal connection in order to sell to consumers.

They use athletes like *Lebron James* to endorse their drink, and obviously Lebron get's paid millions to do so, however, the audience watching who can relate to their passion of basketball have now established a connection with Sprite, and because Sprite now has a personal connection based on your passion for basketball, and uses Lebron James as the advocate it makes it much easier to sell to you and your more inclined to buy.

Show Genuine Interest

By showing genuine interest in others you validate or acknowledge their existence. This simple tactic of displaying some curiosity will help you become more likeable among your peers. People love indulging in themselves by talking about themselves, and by showing genuine interest you give them the opportunity to share their personal life's experiences.

Disclose Your Shortcoming First

You want to admit to your mistakes before you point out the mistakes of others. This works so well psychologically because when you start off by pointing out that you're not a perfect human sub-consciously people around you will think it's ok if they're imperfect as well, and therefore when you bring up their mistakes they will not be offended and are more inclined to accept your criticism constructively.

By sharing your own vulnerabilities first, you create a safe haven for people to reciprocate and share their own shortcomings as well. By doing this you can stop people from going into defensive mode and continue a productive conversation.

Vested Interest of Others

If you want to influence others their own personal interests must be met. People want to be served plain and simple, and by putting other's interests before your own agenda you show people that they're important. A famous salesman by the name of Zig Ziglar once said "You *can get everything in life you want if you will just help enough other people get what they want*". This is coming from a perspective of servitude and by serving others' needs first you can have your needs met as well after you have served enough people. Subconsciously people are usually self-seeking in nature and are always wondering "what's in it for me?". Ergo, the importance of knowing your peers' vested interest.

Create Agreement

Earlier we discussed the theory of cognitive dissonance, and we know that people dislike discord. People are more inclined to congruence and harmony. By getting people to say "yes" to us psychologically speaking they are more inclined to accept your propositions. But in order to do this you need to do so incrementally, and first you want to make them agree to the miniscule things before pitching them the main course. In a sense its like serving them a delightful appetizer before serving them the main meal. Or you can think of it in terms of giving them a soft-ball pitch before giving them a baseball pitch, and in this way, you subtly escalate them from saying yes to the smaller things before saying yes to the bigger things.

Subtly Establish the Standard

Another subtle way of influencing people is by creating a reputation or standard for them to live up too. Humans conform to the identity they have shaped over the course of their life, however by establishing a reputation to live up to people sub-consciously accept that this picture you painted for them is who they are and is their true potential. A great example of this is when you're disciplining your kids, and instead of only telling them the consequences of they're actions you need to tell them you expect better from them because they have so much potential to do better.

By framing this standard, you create the desire for a person to change their behavior because although they have done something wrong initially, you have now established that they have a greater potential and must live up to that standard. This gives people a sense of pride and meaning because now they know they have a lot of self-worth and value, and to preserve this perceived value they must change their behavior.

Mention People's Name

People love hearing their names! The importance of calling people by their given names creates a small surge of euphoria, usually when engaging them for the first time. Calling people by their name creates a personal connection, shows acknowledgement, and shows you recognize who they are. The worst thing you can do is forget people's name or maybe say their name is to hard to pronounce. Learn their names! By using people's name in conversation its like you hit a sweet spot every time and they're more inclined to talk to you and be receptive to your message.

Understanding The Universal Constants

Humans Inherently Selfish?

Developmental theorists argue that humans are born inherently egocentric. Babies, when they take birth, are fully dependent on their mothers. They tend to believe that the mother is their sole savior and the root of all things around them. As the child progresses through life and grows older, it slowly detaches itself from the mother's influence. The person figures out that the mother is truly not the root of all things around him or her and sets out on a new journey.

Many renowned psychologists argue that selfishness and self-centeredness are correlated and synonymous to each other in the behavioral pattern. They are not two different personality traits but, in many ways, the same. Freud used to call it "Her Majesty; the baby." The Tyrant-like figures are common characters in arts, cinema, politics, and work. The majesty rules over a great deal of our unconscious mind. When we are possessed by the majesty, we are often selfish and self-centered without even a hint of guilt.

Need for Companionship

This answer is the most obvious one; we seek companionship because it provides us with the evolutionary advantage. A long, long time ago, a lot of our energy was concentrated towards one goal alone, -survival. Kill this, eat that, stay away from them, and rest here. Be always on your guard, keep your ears out for strange noises and remain vigilant at all times. Move in groups and packs; it is easier to survive that way.

Our present day is no different. Our needs have changed to a certain degree. We don't feel the need to be as alert. Our brains have developed rapidly, we are now capable of amazing scientific breakthroughs, and truly, not as many things require us to be worried about our survival. Hence, we resort to social interaction. We want to keep our brains occupied. That should explain, to a large extent, our obsession with social media.

All of them are elaborate mediums for humans to socialize, to keep themselves from getting bored. New people often interest us. It doesn't matter how intelligent we might be; we are incapable of completely understanding a new person and figuring them all out.

It is no secret that we all are very afraid of being left alone. We as a species dread loneliness and despise it. Our brain is capable of psychoanalyzing and understanding human nature.

The technology we wield brings out just that-loneliness; a form of mass-loneliness where everybody chooses to remain alone while being together at the same time.

There is a sense of inter-connectedness, but it is all artificial. Every single service, transaction and interaction has exclusively gone online, and it is very frightening. The deeper we go down the rabbit hole, the scarier and lonelier it gets. We have many urges that force us to seek companionship.

Another human is only a medium through which we validate ourselves. The point is: we have gradually evolved to seek companionship, and our under-challenging lifestyle and need to seek our true purpose in life have forced us to look for an appropriate companion for life.

Need for money

Money is an invisible hand, which influences human behavior. Money is a tangible form of psychological reassurance of our safety. We all want our future secure and safe, in the event of any unforeseen calamity. Money provides that. If we could see the things that money provides, without the usage of money, we wouldn't value money as much. In fact, there are many places, where currency is still not used. This proves that humans are not attached to these bank notes in particular, but the value they provide.

Our obsession with money is truly an individual choice. It depends on what or how much we need to accumulate to be content and happy in life. The answer to this question depends on the person. Does a BMW make you happy? Or does a private jet make you happy? Does helping your wife cook the food and helping your kids with their math homework make you happy? You see, happiness is different for each person. Our need for money is related to our definitions of happiness.

The day you know what makes you happy, you can go ahead and put a price tag on it. Happiness related to BMW will cost you, a private jet, even more so. But helping your kids and wife is the kind of happiness, which will cost you next to nothing because it is not of materialistic in nature. Once you know exactly how much money you need to be happy in life, you may go out and get it. We will try to work for money, but not know why. Most of these people look back and realize that they worked in vain for things they did not need.

Need for attention

Once you are loved by someone and cared for, you feel a sense of belonging, compassion, and support. It is often noticed that people with low self-esteem fall victim to this behavioral pattern. These individuals seek constant reassurance that they are loved and wanted to elevate their self-worth. No matter how bad things get or how messed up the situation is, they will expect you to help them. If you are a human being, you will almost certainly expect to be cared for and loved consistently. This is a very fundamental human trait. We are, after-all, a bunch of social animals that have learned to curb its animalistic instincts and impulses.

We want to be constantly entertained by our peers, and we always want someone to hear us out when we feel despair and gloom rearing their ugly heads in our life.

Importance of Charisma

Charisma is a trait that is often overlooked when we look at influencing people. We see charisma at work throughout history and a vital characteristic for leaders throughout the century. Even *Adolf Hitler* understood the importance of charisma and the true power it holds. Think about it one of the world's most homicidal maniacs, dictator and tyrant who mass murdered millions of innocent people through the means of concentrations camps and other devices was able to persuade the German people that his way of thinking was acceptable.

Taking a look at things from the outside it may seem almost inconceivable that a person would come up with the notion of an "ideal race", mass genocide, and ultimately world domination. But history tells the tale of these malicious ideas from a madman coming to pass, and one must wonder how on earth such a psychopathic person came into power? How does someone make anti-Semitism and pro- Aryan principles acceptable in larger society?

Well, there are various other factors that contributed to Hitler's rise from the great depression and a terrible economy, current state of affairs, and his notorious book "*Mein Kampf*", however one of the underlying key facets to Hitler's revolution was in fact his charisma. This is how he was able to effectively influence millions of Germans to adopt his ideologies. He may have not been the most qualified political leader in the arena, however, having infectious charisma helped him come into power.

Nelson Mandela another famous political leader that influenced the world through a more positive and meaningful impact is also thought to be someone who is charismatic. He dismantled segregation going on in South Africa at the time and was able to usher in a new era of unity among people in the nation bringing together people of different races and tearing down cultural taboos.

So now we see two different polar opposite leaders on the spectrum who both used charisma to influence the people around them. But the question now is what is charisma and how can it be quantified? Charisma seems like a more abstract concept hard to grasp and confined to our limited human understanding of the world around us. But from a psychological stand point how can we define this term?

Well, charisma can be thought of as a symbol that is rooted in human values and emotions. By symbol I refer to the representation of values and emotions manifested in a person's conduct or demeanor. This manifestation of charisma is usually something people stand for, believe in, and are passionate about. Ultimately something that can be visibly seen through our body language too.

But what is the underlying framework behind charisma? There are a few elements which make charisma so infectious, and they are as follows; Vision, substance, and presentation.

Vision - When influencing people, you need to create a vision that has an impactful message, powerful imagery through the use of metaphors, and story telling capabilities. You also want to provide a comparison of subject matters, engage your audience with internal thought provoking questions, and reinforce through repetition.

Substance - You must posses well grounded assertions when speaking to your audience that can convince people to trust in you. Elicit rhetorical questions and persuade your audience by captivating messages that can connect with them on a personal level. Your audience should have such conviction that they feel as if you are personally speaking to them 1 on 1. Also, expressing the experiences of collective society and using the means as justification for the ends.

Presentation - The delivery of your message should be enthusiastic and passionate your presentation should utilize strong voice, tone, body language and other techniques to convince your audience. Have you ever seen a speech from Martin Luthor King? If you have you can probably see how Dr. King successfully utilizes his tone, body language and voice to captivate his audience with a historically impactful message that resonates till this day. His presentation skills are so adept that it demands your attention front and centre.

Putting It All together

The importance of social capital cannot be understated, hence why you want to learn how to influence people effectively. The connections you make and the people you encounter in society can greatly enhance the quality of your life, and thus the importance of making meaningful connections and relationships you can leverage to your benefit. Having a solid network of people in your life is a sure way in securing emotional, financial and social stability. But, remember you're not here to manipulate or use and abuse people, however all the relationships you develop should have a mutually beneficial element to it where both parties receive perks and advantages.

You want to provide some type of value and this can take place in many forms whether financial, intellectual, emotional support, or even companionship. Everyone has different perceived values and needs in life and therefore it will differ person to person and case by case basis. The truth is people of the general public are easily impressionable beings and we see this today people being influenced by music, fashion, culture and different mannerisms.

People want to have a belonging in society as humans are social creatures and thrive in tribes or group settings. -It is in our nature to socially interact with one another. You can even say people sub-consciously want to be influenced because after all the mind is like a blank slate ready to be moulded, shaped and influenced by societies' many facets.

Always be mindful of every single encounter you make with a person. If you want to win them over as friends and influence them, you should always consider the following questions; How can I bring value to this conversation or person? How can I establish a commonality or reference point? What does this person want? What do I need to do in order to create a memorable, personal and lasting connection?

Listen Attentively & Paraphrase

As discussed earlier listening and hearing are two terms that are often mistakenly used interchangeably. But what is the importance of listening when influencing people? As you know as previously discussed listening is when you attentively process information consciously and not just "hearing" sound. Whenever you get a chance to respond and you know your cue try paraphrasing the conversation because this reinforces a few things, 1. The person will know you're attentively listening, and you have an understanding of their unique situation, 2. You reinforce inclusivity by affirming the gist of their message and therefore acknowledge the importance of it.

Highlight What Resonates With Them

People you encounter will generally speaking always have their own vested interests at heart. Therefore, it would make sense to have a message that resonates with them that can connect you to them on a more deep and personal level. This could range from anything from a reference point you have identified, common ground, cultural themes, etc.

For instance, you get into a conversation with someone who is a fan of a particular basketball team, and you notice they wear clothing apparel that supports this team such as caps, jerseys and even shoes. What you need to do is strike up conversation with them about their favorite team, and the key here is allow them to do most of the talking. If you don't know much about the team you can easily research it on your smart-phone granted you have a secure WIFI connection. By enabling the person to talk about something they're passionate about you resonate with them on a much more intimate level because they are having conversation with you about something, they hold very dear themselves.

This creates a more positive and memorable experience with people you encounter because they have now created a fond impression about you by default because when they remember you in their thoughts, they will remember their encounter in a positive light because they were doing most the talking and it was something, they were passionate about. Remember allowing people to talk during the majority of the conversation gives a sort of self-validation which all humans look for in one way or another.

Never Direct Blame Towards People

This is one of the most fundamental things you need to know when influencing people! Never direct blame towards people! Let's face it nobody likes to be made the scapegoat or blamed, and by shifting blame towards people directly you are potentially ruining the relationship your trying so hard to build. Blaming people creates fear, resentment, and avoidance behavior.

Blame does not need to be directed towards anyone, however, you can make people aware of their faults but in a subtler fashion. Here is an example, you're the boss of a grocery store and your cashier clerk made errors during his shift that resulted in being short on cash by the end of the day by $50 dollars. Rather than going to him directly and chastising him and calling him out on his mistakes which has incurred your small monetary losses, you should approach him and advise that it appears that during his shift at his cash register there is a report of a $50 discrepancy. Go over the report find the mistake and advise next time he should do things differently in order to prevent financial losses.

Now this pragmatic approach can be applied in almost any situation you encounter. Someone makes mistakes, and rather than using words that ostracize people directly such as "you", instead advise them to do things differently when they encounter the same situation. Explain the cause and effect relationship related to their mistake and advise what can be done differently the next time. By doing this you preserve the relationship with your employee, build rapport, creates more trust, and he or she may be more inclined to have further questions to your benefit, and ultimately your able to influence them a lot easier because now you have garnered their respect because you've dealt with them professionally and not harshly.

Create Thought Provoking Conversation

In order to captivate people, you need not only have a message that resonates with them, but you want them to question their own framework of prevailing ideologies, values, social norms and customs. The conversation you have with them must have substance, create curiosity and builds rapport. Not the typical, "Hi, how was your day?" type of responses, however you want to engage people you encounter on a much more personal level by identifying what they're passionate about and letting them talk about themselves.

Now this doesn't mean you have to have some intrinsically deep and philosophical theme emanating from all your conversations, but you want to be able to make people question their own believe systems by enlightening them with a new perspective.

What if you encounter an intellectual? Well, not worry you can discuss more pragmatic philosophies such as what is the "true meaning of life" the ever burning question that has existed since humans walked the earth. Allow them to respond, and when its your cue to input your answer simply say, "the meaning of life is up to each individual as a person to discover and embellish meaning to one's own life through experience, learning, pain, joy, hurt, love, and passion." This is just an example of possible response to a thought provoking questions you may encounter with different people you meet.

Importance of Commonality and Reference Point

When engaging someone you need to quickly asses and identify a point of reference where you can build common ground. This point of common ground is what builds rapport for the longer term, for instance in a previous example I mentioned seeing someone in attire that indicates they are sports fans for a certain team. You know this because the clothing apparel they are wearing indicates a franchise team such as jersey, shoes, caps, etc. From this point of reference, you want to start talking about that particular sport whether its NFL, NBA, NHL, etc.

Thus, you allow rapport building to take place and now have an engaged recipient in your conversation who is more inclined to talk to you about personal matters and has an affinity towards you. Again, remember to allow the person to do most of the talking as this serves to self-validate themselves and acknowledge their importance.

Never disagree Always Understand & Acknowledge Their Perspectives

The biggest mistakes I see today by people in authority who by trade need to influence people is blatantly disagreeing with their audience. We see politicians do it all the time! Instead of taking the time to acknowledge and understand the other side they go on the offensive and belittle, tear down, and create conflict among their peers. When you decide to disagree with someone you create disharmony and as mentioned earlier in the psychology chapter humans don't like discord or conflict, however people tend to gravitate towards harmony and unity.

Am I telling you to be a sell out? Absolutely not! But I am saying when you're in a disagreement you need to act in a subtler fashion as oppose to going in guns blazing or being a loose cannon. The truth is you can still influence people who may otherwise disagree with your stance or ideologies, hence, you can win them over through inclusive body language and professionalism. Some people may not resonate with your core messages, but they can be drawn towards your charisma, body language and professional conduct. They may think "Although I don't really accept his side of the argument, he's been able to conduct himself professionally, shows vibrant character and positive body language."

What if you encounter controversial topics or debates? Well, generally speaking I admonish you to steer clear from these types of conversations because this can get quite dicey and you can potentially open up a plethora of problems. But if you have no choice but to engage you want to do so in a polite and diplomatic fashion. -Diplomacy is key. You can say something like "I understand your perspective and acknowledge your stance, however my beliefs are contrary….." , and from there you just fill in the blanks of the topic at hand.

You don't want to create hostility or resentment or position yourself as someone who is in higher authority. However, you want to show that the person you talk to is your equal and both of you can diplomatically agree to disagree. Humility helps in these types of volatile conversations because once the other side sees your someone who is down to earth and practical they become much more docile.

Conclusion

Congratulations! You've reached the end of the book! You've learned body language fundamentals, historical psychological theories, personality types, dark human psychology, how to assess and read people, and influence them as well. You are now ready to go out and become a proficient practioner of analyzing people in our society. You've learned the inner workings and machinations of a psychologist's mind, and you've even learned the framework behind the world's greatest fictional detective *Sherlock Homles*, using both deductive and inductive reasoning and many other faculties of psychology.

Don't expect to instantly be a professional practioner of analyzing people. The more people you encounter and engage you'll notice the better you get. This is both a skill and craft that needs to be practiced and implemented daily in order to get better at it.

With all this said I want to leave you with a *gift*! This book couldn't be complete without giving you **bonus chapters!** Within these bonuses chapters I have as always provided illustrated diagrams of examples on how you can analyze people, diagram dissections, and more theories on practical psychology. I hope you enjoy these bonus chapters!

Wishing you all the best,

Jason Gale

Bonus Section Chapters

Facial Expression Analysis & Interpretation:

*Note, some people may be better at masking their emotions than others, so use this info as a guiding template and general rule of thumb, but with discretion. Perhaps not all mentioned facial expression will be revealed, but a few of them will, which still indicates expression of the emotion.

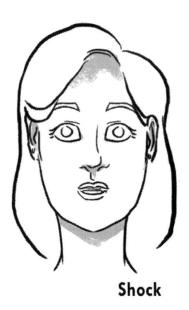

Shock

Shock:

Shock is a powerful emotion and can be elicited through various stimulates. Usually caused by something sudden or unexpected which creates a burst of awe in the recipient on the receiving end of the information.

How can you tell someone is "shocked"? From a body language stance and facial expression view point, one can observe people who undergo the emotion of shock exhibit quite a few indicative facial expressions.

Diagram Dissection:

As you can see "shock" manifesting physically through facial expressions in the above diagram. Characterized by exaggerated raised eye brows, widened eye lids and dilated pupils. Also notice the mouth, opened slightly, and carefully observe the nose as nostrils expand as well.

When looking for shock analyze these key traits in facial expression and you'll be able to discover if a person is shocked or not.

Deception

Deception:

On the other end of the emotional spectrum, deception is a character trait that is frowned upon and considered one of the more cunning human characteristics that exists within our emotional psychology. Often thought to be a flawed characteristic in a person and prime indicator of a sociopath.

There are various scenarios in everyday life where deception can come into play in different degrees. People may tend to use this trait to better themselves at the expense of others. For instance, a sales representative closes a sale using deception, business transactions conducted through deception, and dishonest gains made through deception. In these scenarios someone stoops so low to use unethical means to get what they want.

The sales rep could grossly exaggerate the functions and capabilities of the product that is being sold. In the business transaction example the business man could of used shady tactics to close the deal. As you can see there are different scenarios in life where deception is utilized.

Diagram Dissection:

Deception may be one of the hardest traits to detect through facial expression, but there are significant signs to look out for. Observe the eyes and look for rapid or unusual blinking. Usually when someone is not telling the truth they tend to blink abnormally. Also, a key indicator to look for is a straight and emotionless face, you'll notice someone putting in more effort than usual to keep a calm and compose demeanor.

Above you can see lips are usually locked as the person will try to use as little facial expression as possible to fly under the radar and to convey calmness. One of the most crucial signs to analyze and watch out for is breathing. Observe breathing patterns; is it shallow or rapid? Usually shallow or rapid breathing indicates that the person is uncomfortable or trying to hide something.

Jealousy

Jealously:

Considered one of the more dangerous and detrimental emotions, jealously. If left unchecked this negative emotion can destroy your life or seriously effect others around you. The basis of jealousy is found in coveting, desiring what someone else has. This is not exclusive only to materialistic things, although more often than not it does encompass such, but it could also be translated into the real world by being jealous of physical appearance, affiliations, social status, etc.

Often the jealous person is self-absorbed and likes to compare one's self worth to others. He/she is never content and has this sort of entitlement mentality, thinking only he/she deserves the best of what life has to offer.

Diagram Dissection:

Jealously is a emotion that can be easily seen with the trained eye. Visibly seen through facial expression, observe the diagram and see the collapsed eye brows, one will be raised slightly higher than the other, a slight grin ("fake smile"), and an intense glare. Eye lids will be squinted or wide open, and the pupils in both eyes will be dilated.

Also, watch for conversational cues that indicate jealously. For instance, perhaps you got a new car or received a promotion in your job. Someone who is jealous usually does not wish you well or genuinely congratulates you on your accomplishments. However, they will be the first to subtly criticize your achievements and question your success. Thus, observe and listen carefully!

Empathy

Empathy:

Considered a personality trait among the compassionate and this is a virtue that is treasured among the noblest of people. Being able to put yourself in someone else's shoes is a rare ability, especially in this day and age given the narcissistic and self-absorbed society we find ourselves faced with.

Diagram Dissection

Facial expressions of empathetic people which reveal this emotional trait are easily visible. A inclusive, calm and welcoming demeanor is present, eye brows are leveled evenly, an authentic smile, and most of all a listening ear.

Eyes glow with compassion and show genuine concern as oppose to contempt. Empathetic people are ones who are quick to listen and slow to speak, and put others first. There are varying levels of empathy and different people are at different stages. For instance, people who have the ability to empathize on a higher level tend to have some sort of common relatability on a personal level, and a emotional or sentimental value that distinguishes one personal connection from another.

Lower level empaths connect on a more superficial level and have a general understanding of someone's suffering, but cannot connect on a personal level. There is a lack of a personal and deep emotional connection, which is due to absent experiences.

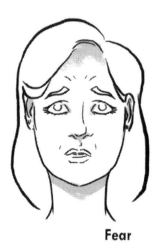

Fear

Fear:

Perhaps one of the most archaic and baser emotions that has existed since humans walked the earth. Throughout history we can see this baser emotion being exploited through religion, dictators, ideologies and politics. Fear is a central theme among all societies and peoples from all walks of life.

Diagram Dissection:

Fear is probably the most visible and easily interpreted emotion that manifests through our facial expression. It's an emotion that is difficult to hide from others. Take a look at the diagram above; indented forehead, raised and quaking eye brows, gaping mouth, and dilated pupils. Other key indicators not shown on the diagram could be trembling legs or arms, and irregular breathing patterns.

This is probably one of easiest emotions to spot and even someone who is inexperienced in analyzing can easily detect fear in people.

Understanding Culture

Human beings thrive on social interaction and cannot function at optimum potential without it, case in point the complex and diverse phenomenon known as culture. All cultures have their rudimentary roots and have been cumulated from generation to generation, being passed down from one genesis to another.

The essential components to any given culture constitute symbols, values, norms and production. Values are simply a standard of behaviors that are followed within a given culture; through this a culture defines what is good or bad, desirable or ugly. Symbols are used in the realm of culture to signify certain things, for example a cross represents the crucifixion of the Christian Savior.

Values produce norms, thus if values is what defines good and bad, traditions and customs would stem from values being catered toward the perception of what good and bad is from a given culture.

Since the dawn of the scientific revolution, society is advancing in terms of knowledge, medicine, and technology. We live in a society that is heavily dependent on empirical evidence, facts, and track records. Which isn't a bad thing. Although it is worth noting particular cultural beliefs and even traditions have changed over the course of time in inverse proportions as society as a whole evolves itself by embellishing in greater knowledge.

Remember cultures hold different values and beliefs of what is right and wrong. But we must question who decides what path is the right one? And how do you recognize somebody who strays from it? Where does this knowledge come from? The ability to know right and wrong, these are merely artificial constructs determined by those who are in positions of authority who adjudicate or impose their beliefs on others, usually subordinates.

Like a blank canvas is a human needing to be refined, defined and molded. Influenced and shaped by environmental context and experiences. Imagine a canvas waiting to be painted by the color of cultural values and norms. This can be thought of like an analogy proportionate to how cultures, values and norms arise. When born into existence we are like clean slates, but through passage of time we gain experiences and assimilate cultural values and norms.

Mindset : Abundance Vs Scarcity

We all want to be successful, right? Becoming the greatest versions of ourselves is what we should all strive for at the least. We owe it to ourselves to live life to its fullest capacity and get the most out of it. Investing in yourself is the first step, and I want to congratulate you on taking the first step to investing in yourself by purchasing this book! Now in this bonus chapter I'd like to discuss mindset and the importance of conditioning your mind the right way.

So in this world there are three kinds of people, either you have an abundance mindset or suffer from a scarcity mentality or your somewhere in between. Now a lot of people in this day and age suffer from what I like to call a scarcity mindset, meaning these people are extremely cynical, fearful, stingy, and want to stay in their comfort zone. These kinds of people are stubborn, not willing to change, and want to live life in their little bubble. They feel the world owes them and have this type of entitlement complex.

Then there are people who have an abundance mindset who's characteristics are as follows tenacious, motivated, gives freely, optimistic and adapts to any environment. I'd like to try out an experiment with you, picture a glass of water its filled half way, now I want you to tell me is the cup half full or half empty? Based on your answer we can derive what type of mentality you posses! If you answered half full, it's likely you suffer from a scarcity mindset, however if you choose half empty you most likely have an abundance mindset.

This is more or less an analogy and open to interpretation, but generally speaking people who suffer from a scarcity mindset tend to view the world and its resources as scarce, but people with the abundance mentality always look at the world as plentiful, with room to grow and believe the sky is the limit. The difference between the two mentalities is diametric and identifying which one you have can go a long way. It's obvious the more favorable and advantageous mentality is abundance, and all you need to do is assimilate this mindset into your life by shifting your perception to start looking at the world as your oyster filled with opportunities, only if you're willing to look.

If your struggling with a scarcity mindset chances are its effecting certain aspects of your life, perhaps you don't even realize it. Abundance and scarcity mindsets can translate into almost every aspect of life whether jobs, finance, dating, etc. It really comes down to being optimistic versus pessimistic. Let's take a look below at some examples and dissect some scenarios where we can see the scarcity mindset at work.

Jobs

An anti-social employee who only looks out for himself. He likes to be the centre of attention, shifts blame when he's at fault, often gossips about other co workers, refuses to train new employees and although talented at his craft remains at the same job for over 10 years.

Lets break down this scenario. This employee exhibits firstly an inferiority complex (low self esteem) which can be associated with his anti-social antics. He does not owe up to his mistakes or take responsibility. He refuses to train other employees properly due to the fear of the new employee becoming better than him, and lastly remains stagnant at the same job for a decade, although he is talented in his craft and has the capability to move up, therefore this indicates the fear of losing his current job or the fear of not finding something better.

We can sum up all his negative traits to possessing a scarcity mindset. People with this mindset will be selfish, resentful to others, fearful and complacent with what they have. In this example we can see an employee who lives in constant fear of losing his job, scared of other colleagues surpassing him, and simply just limited by his own beliefs.

Finance

There are a lot of people out there who make a substantial amount of money, but they are afraid to invest that money. Investing doesn't just mean "stocks", we all know there are risks associated with that, but what I am referring to is investing in oneself by buying books, courses and going to seminars. These people tend to be stingy, clingy and simply put misers. This simply stems from the fact that they do not want to lose what they earned or perhaps view spending the money as wasting.

A good example would be a wealthy business man needing a new pair of shoes as they got worn out over the years from wear and tear. But, he refused to buy himself new shoes because he views it as a waste of money and thinks of better ways he could spend his money.

Again, we can see the scarcity mentality operating here and dictating the financial decisions this business man makes. The scarcity mentality is limiting his spending habits in a detrimental way, and he simply holds onto money for the sake of it. He has the financial capacity to easily purchase himself a dozen pairs of shoes, but he doesn't want to even spend it on one pair! People like this hold onto money just for the sake of it sadly, and unfortunately their money does no good beyond the grave.

People like this who have this clenches fist mentality towards money are limiting their growth, although they me be financially well off they eliminate any chance of growth because of their scarcity mentality. What happens is due to their reluctant approach they close themselves off to new   opportunities, and it's not until they are willing to open their fist and let go, that more abundance will come into their lives.

Dating

Yes, scarcity can even be found in dating! Have you ever come across clingy or desperate people? What kind of vibe do they exude? Definitely one that deters you. Imagine in this scenario a girl is in a relationship with a guy, and she constantly calls to check up on him, nonstop text messages, always wants to be around him, and her whole life revolves around her boyfriend. Eventually the boyfriend is suffocated in desperation, he has no choice but to end the relationship for his own well being.

Can you see the scarcity mindset at work here? The clinginess, desperation and just outright neediness is displayed. The female in this relationship seems to have built her whole universe around her significant other to the extent of literally suffocating him!

This can arise due to a few reasons, she has this notion that she won't find someone else, scared of losing her significant other, and just being limited in her options for dating. Clearly, she is in disbelief that they're "plenty of fish" in the sea as they say. Instead of cherishing the moment, allowing the freedom of her significant other to come and go as he pleases, she instead obstructed his life. Once a person has the self determination to go and come at will only then will he/she be willing to stay in a relationship. It's like holding a butterfly in your hand, appreciating its beauty and allowing it to fly. Can you see the parallel? In this case she clenched her fist and suffocated the butterfly, ultimately destroying the relationship.

Consciousness & Analyzing

Consciousness is one of the most controversial and debated topics of the century. It is a intangible substance and exists in the realm of the abstract. Its metaphysical nature is what makes this topic so controversial and at times hard to grasp. It cannot be computed by mathematics, indescribable by physicists or biologists, but yet undeniably recognized as an entity that exists in each person.

But for the purpose of this book we will define consciousness as the awareness of self, reality and environment. This enables us to gather information, discern, and organize it all at once. Consciousness allows us to contemplate life, create ideas, design concepts, analyze and be creative.

Through conscious analyzing we are enabled to plan for the future, reminisce on our past, and consider outcomes and consequences of certain actions.

Within our daily lives we must recognize our various conscious states that occur spontaneously, such as sleeping, being awake, dreaming, meditating and drug induced states. It is believed that everything that occurs on the psychological level also has a simultaneous biologically occurring reaction, and in this case, activity in our brains. There are different layers of consciousness that have been discovered over the century, and I'd like to discuss one layer that is considered a dual process functioning consciousness and this is in relation to analyzing. Please see below.

Deliberate Mind

This is a more practical functioning layer of consciousness that we engage with on a daily basis. For instance, imagine you are at a park and see a bird, you only see it at face value meaning you identified the object, surroundings and are aware of the species.

Automatic Mind

This layer of consciousness operates simultaneously along side with the "deliberate mind", however functions like a sub-processor similar to a computer, and gathers specific information that entails subjective facts, perception, and details surrounding the reality you are viewing.

In the example of the bird in the park we saw the deliberate mind interpreting information at face value. On the contrary the automatic mind would gather information in regards to the following; color, height, distance, movement, and personal associations.

Selective Attention

So now you must be wondering how do we keep our focus with all this "noise" and various processes going on in the background of our minds? We do this through something called selective attention, which is the focus of our consciousness on one specific stimulus and through which we filter out all the background noise in our minds. Imagine our consciousness like a spotlight on a crowded stage, we focus the attention on one particular person, thus drawing attention to one certain stimuli at a time. This analogy reveals how selective attention works, which is by focusing on the relevant and tuning out irrelevant information, which in this case is whoever is not in the spotlight at the time. Everyone else on the crowded stage would just fade in the background, while our focus remains on the specific stimuli that is under the "spotlight".

Correlation Does Not Mean Causality

A famous coined term used by a lot of statisticians is "correlation does not mean causation ". But what does this mean? Just because two phenomenon are closely related to one another, this does not imply causation. A correlation can be defined as the direction or degree of association between two variables. A correlation between two variables can arise due to a third factor involved in a phenomenon. Meaning this third factor or variable could in fact be the very cause of the third variable.

In order to accurately arrive to a definitive conclusion one must be cognizant of all the various variables in any given phenomenon in order to correctly establish correlation and an event. For instance, stores exponentially increase in sales during cold winter months compared to summer months. Do we draw an inference and make a blanket assessment stating there is a cause and effect relationship between cold weather and increased sales? Certainly not, and it may even seem somewhat paradoxical that cold weather causes people to spend more money, as during that season of the year people tend to be confined indoors.

What is the missing link or factor? Well, at a closer glance we can associate another variable which is "holiday celebrations", such as Christmas and New Years. People will spend more money not because of the cold weather, but because of these traditional and national holiday celebrations where materialistic goods get the most advertisements, discount prices, and bargains. These holidays, Christmas in particular is heavily saturated with materialism, and the increase in sales associated to Christmas is indisputable. As you can see this is a perfect classical example of how correlation does not necessarily mean causation in the grand scheme of things. So, linking cold weather to increased sales for stores is not an accurate depiction of correlation and causation, as we found out that there was a third variable involved that was the driving factor in sales.

How does this relate to analyzing people? Now you're aware of the fundamentals of correlation and causation, when analyzing people you now know not to make quick blanket assessments without seeing the entire picture. So, giving someone the benefit of the doubt would be the appropriate thing to do. As you know there are a plethora of factors that can cause a person to act a certain way. For example, you run into your best friend at the store whom you haven't seen in years and he seems indifferent towards you, gives you no eye contact when talking, and just storms out the store. Do you now make an assessment stating this individual was rude, inconsiderate, and ultimately not a good friend?

Later you found out that this best friend of yours was running late for an important appointment which took months to schedule. Now we see a third variable surface in perfect clarity, thus a correct appraisal would be he was running late for an appointment, had no time to talk, and had to leave the store as soon as humanly possible. This has nothing to do with him not being a good friend or rude, and as you can see case in point correlation does not mean causation.

Measuring Personalities

How would you describe your personality? Perhaps kind, timid, quirky, creative or friendly? People have been characterizing each other's personalities for a long time through different theories of categorization and some probably more accurate than others. This all really boils down to one burning question, and that's who or what is the self? To be concise the self can be considered a collective organization of thoughts, feelings, and actions. This in essence forms the core of all our personalities. Below is an example of two fundamental types of perceptions of the "self".

Ideal Self - Popular, successful, loved, financially secure, and emotionally stable.

Feared Self- Unemployed, failure, alone, and an emotional wreck.

We must first start of by looking at various characteristic and how these combined characteristics establish a unique whole thinking and emotional being. This drive to measure personality by many psychologist is met with a road block, and that is you cannot really quantify an intangible substance through an empirical approach. Personalities are dynamic in nature and can range from one side of the spectrum to the other. However, we have come up with a few ways in measuring personality types.

We can look to define personality through stable lasting behavior patterns, and conscious motivations. We can use certain personality traits such as calmness, impulsiveness, cynical, trusting, practical, creative, fearful and brave to predict behaviors and attitudes. For example an introvert would prefer to communicate via e-mail as oppose to face to face contact, as oppose to a confident person who is comfortable communicating face to face.

However, it must be noted that this is not necessarily black and white as there can be other factors involved in the expression of certain personality traits. For instance, someone who is introverted and dislikes one on one communication with people might actually feel comfortable speaking to large audiences. How can this be? Well, measuring personalities are not an exact science, however, depending on right environmental conditions the expression or suppression of certain personalities traits can occur. So it would be fair to say human's posses a degree of flexibility when it comes to personality, and these traits are not fixed, rigid or set in stone, but can be changed.

There is another way of measuring personality and that is by comparing interaction of traits and their social context. We learn a lot of behaviors by observing and emulating others, but we are also aware of the various social interactions that affect our behaviors. Thus, people and their situations work in tandem to create behavior. Meaning the books you read, music you listen to, sports you play, and friends you hang out with dictate the type of personality you have. This can be considered a type of social conditioning where the influences within your social context mould the framework of who you are.

People for the most part choose what type of social context to be in, and the social context in turn reinforces our personality types. This is so profound as in this way humans are both the creators and products of the social context we surround ourselves with! Thus, this school of thought indicates our sense of personal control, which means your perception on how much control you have over your social context and environment. People who believe they control their own fate and create their own destiny are said to have an " internal point of control", and those who designate external forces as controllers of their lives are said to have a " external point of control".

Truth About Intelligence

We've all heard it before " He's is so smart" or " She is so intelligent". But what do we really attribute intelligence to? Defining intelligence is a complicated thing, and it is not restricted to specific labels or frameworks. The fact is intelligence can be measured in so many ways, and there are different types of intelligences that exist. It's not like height, weight or anything that you can measure with precision.

It holds different meanings for different cultures, ages and skill sets. Although the complexity of defining intelligence can be seen, we can start to understand it more thoroughly by posing questions such as how can it be assessed and what influences it? Is it confined to singular abilities and restricted to certain tasks? Or does it have a variety of aptitudes, skills and talents? What about innovation, creativity and art?

There are many factors that come into play such as genetics, environment and access to resources (education). We can loosely define intelligence as the aptitude to learn from experiences, adapt to new situations and problem solve. I think we can all agree intelligence goes beyond retaining information from a text book for extended periods of time to only forget it within 6 months, after exam time.

We often use intelligent tests (IQ) to gauge current levels of aptitude. But, these test can only gauge one dimensional aspects of intelligence, and totally forget about other types of intelligence, such as creativity, innovation and art.

What if you were an extremely talented painter, but couldn't comprehend basic mathematics or posses inadequate spelling capabilities. Does this mean your intelligent or not? Interesting fact, did you know people who suffer from savant syndrome excel exceptionally well in computation or drawing? Yet, these people tend to be socially awkward and "abnormal" according to societies standards. The fact is traditional IQ test cannot really provide accurate and definitive answers to what intelligence really is, despite what your teachers might say.

For instance how can you quantify creativity on a IQ test? You can't. There is no standardized test that can measure creativity, innovation and art.

This is quite a controversial subject as well, but standardized testing is not an accurate indicator on someone's intelligence let alone determine the success of an individual. As we previously discussed intelligence is multifaceted and there are so many aspects to it, and designed standardized test does society a disservice, and only seems to stigmatize, label and categorize groups of people. Usually people who come from lower socio-economic statuses fall on the lower end of the spectrum. But, how can you justify their inaccessibility to resources (education) and fairly equate that to their capacity in life?

Its nonsensical. There is a definitive correlation between people who come from poorer lower income families and their scarcity to access educational resources as oppose to those who come from affluence. Standardized testing may be able to gauge the current skill set of an individual, but in no way is a life sentence or conclusive of intelligence as a whole.

Emotion Dynamics

Perceiving emotions - being able to instantly recognize emotions in face to face contact, stories, films, and music.

Understanding Emotions - The ability to predict emotions and forecast how they may change.

Managing Emotions - Expressing yourself appropriately proportionate to the context or situation you find yourself in.

Emotions and the way we express them can be awkward, strange and yet profoundly powerful. Emotions are not transient psychological phenomenon, but can actually effect our health and state of well being. The power of positive or negative emotions are stronger than you can imagine, after all it is through our emotions we've all made some sort of impulsive decisions.

It's quite a known fact that people who people who have a positive set of emotions live good, long and fulfilling lives, while their counter parts live in regret, misery and sorrow. Emotions such as fear and anger tend to be provoked by stress, and before we can learn to truly harness our emotions, we must learn how to understand them.

The truth is some people are better at reading emotions than others. We previously discussed the differences between introverts and extroverts in the beginning of this book. Introverts tend to gravitate towards understanding emotions better, while extroverts are really good at expressing their emotions.

Emotions are in essence the conscious experiences of what we are feeling at that current state and moment in time. Take a look below at universal emotions displayed across all cultures around the world.

Universal Emotions

Joy

Surprise

Anger

Contempt

Shame

Fear

Sadness

Surprise

Guilt

Disgust

Love

Pride

Excitement

These polarities of emotions go beyond realm of psychology. They are far reaching and as mentioned before can affect our physiology and various biochemical mechanisms within the body. When it comes to the more negative spectrum of emotions we often overestimate the duration of these "bad times" and underestimate our ability to adapt. Every single emotion we have has the capacity to build and simmer or activate with great crippling intensity.

Analyzing Stress

We've all experienced stressful events in our lives in some way, shape or form in varying capacities and intensities. Stress is not considered an emotion but, an irritation as a result of an external stimulus. However, reactions are completely dependent on how a recipient perceives the stimulus. There are three main modules we can categorize stress within such as small scale, medium scale and large scale.

Large scale - War, famine, epidemics, and natural disasters.

Medium scale - Life changes; moving, new child, death of a loved one, divorce or a new job.

Micro scale - inconveniences, traffic, running late, exam prep, etc.

Regardless of what stress you face whether big or small it can still activate our fight our "flight response". Therefore, you must realize stress is a normal part of life! Its natural, but it only becomes a problem when its excess. Similar to how muscle growth occurs under some sort of stressful stimulus, and in this case some sort of resistances caused by a weight that puts "stress" on your muscle. Normal stress can be thought to function much in the same manner.

Healthy Stress - Makes you alert, active and can boost your immune system.

Chronic Stress - This type of stress is the kind you don't want. With chronic stress you are more susceptible to digestive, respiratory, and infectious diseases. -And let's not forget emotional instability.

Next we will take a look at personality disorders and learn how to spot and understand them.

Analyzing Personality Disorders

What are personality disorders? These are marked by inflexible, obsessive, and disruptive social behavioral patterns that affect basic social functioning skills. Personality disorders can take many forms, and can be subtle or extremely noticeable. Nonetheless, they can affect a person's life considerably and the one suffering may not even recognize he/she possesses a personality disorder.

These disorders range on the spectrum from lacking empathy towards others to egotistical narcissism. Most these extreme disorders fall into two categories that you've probably heard of, which are psychopathic or sociopathic. History has been littered with notorious individuals with psychopathic or sociopathic tendencies that have came into positions of power, such as Genghis Khan, Adolf Hitler, Vlad The Impaler, Jack The Ripper, Stalin and the list goes on, and on.

Personalities have been studied by various cultures over the century, but the concept of personality disorders is a relatively new idea. Below are examples of personality disorders we find within our society.

Anti-Social - Engages in behavior that opposes societal norms, values and basic principles.

Eccentric - Quirky or odd. Unusual behavior, paranoid, constantly suspicious and distrusts almost everyone.

Narcissistic - Focused only on self-interest, self-important and possesses a strong sense of entitlement.

Histrionic - Attention seeking, even at the risk of one's own life.

Avoidant - Characterized by fear, avoidance and social anxiety. Lacks confidence and clingy.

Personality disorders is a diverse group psychological conditions determined by various variables. The truth is psychologists only have recently really begun to understand personality disorders, and there is still much more to learn.

Social Thinking

Have you ever wondered how dictators or tyrants come into power? Or even how bullies can treat someone with such cruelty? Well, in this bonus chapter we will discuss social psychology which focuses situations, influences and how we collectively think in certain conditions.

Humanity as a whole is capable of great things, but at the same time has painted itself with a dark past in how we dehumanize others. So, when people do things whether good or bad, we must inquire did they commit such actions because of their personality or situation? Thus, is someone's behavior based on personal disposition or circumstantial?

The answer is it's a combination of both! Sometimes the power of a particular circumstantial situation can easily override personality. You can think of it as a sort of peer pressure effect where the circumstantial situation influences behavior. But, then again history shows us a lot of personality dispositional behaviors despite strong environmental norms. For instance, helping Jewish families escape the Nazi genocide or assisting the escape of African American slaves through the underground rail road. We can see personality disposition, in specific altruistic behaviors at work here despite the dark miasma.

GET YOUR AUDIO-BOOK BUNDLE SET ABSOLUTELY FREE !

HOW TO ANALYZE PEOPLE QUICKLY, FACIAL EXPRESSIONS,
PSYCHOLOGY,BODY LANGUAGE, AND BEHAVIORS:
ULTIMATE GUIDE

Link Below:

http://analyze.healthypslife.com

Printed in Great Britain
by Amazon